Forest School Adventure

Forest School Adventure

Outdoor Skills and Play for Children

Naomi Walmsley & Dan Westall

FSC
www.fsc.org
MIX
Paper from
responsible sources
FSC® C020056

First published 2018 by
Guild of Master Craftsman
Publications Ltd, Castle Place,
166 High Street, Lewes,
East Sussex BN7 1XU

Reprinted 2018

Text © Dan Westall and Naomi
Walmsley, 2018. Copyright in
the Work © GMC Publications
Ltd, 2018

ISBN 978 1 78494 403 2

The publishers and author can accept no legal
responsibility for any consequences arising from
the application of information, advice
or instructions given in this publication.

A catalogue record for this book is available from
the British Library.

Publisher Jonathan Bailey
Production Manager Jim Bulley
Senior Project Editor Virginia Brehaut
Editor Nicola Hodgson
Managing Art Editor Gilda Pacitti
Designer Manisha Patel
Illustrator Sarah Skeate

Colour origination by GMC Reprographics
Printed and bound in China

Contents

Introduction

Packed full of practical ideas for getting kids outside, this book is your essential companion for helping them play, craft and learn about the natural world around us. Make fire by rubbing sticks together, build a shelter to sleep under, create stone tools using sandstone and slate, make natural glue from tree sap, harvest clay from the earth to make pots, make common garden weeds into delicious and nourishing wild food and much more.

When we met, one of the things that drew us together was our shared connection with nature and our passion for living and working outdoors. As children, we were often late home and covered in dirt from building dens, climbing trees and exploring caves. Some things don't change: we still arrive home late and are covered in dirt after a session in our woodland! We have been teaching in the outdoors for many years, but our greatest learning experience, which shaped the way we live and teach now, was a wilderness adventure in the mountains and cedar forests of eastern Washington, USA, taking part in a five-month course living as primitive hunter-gatherers.

We quit our jobs, said goodbye to our lives in the UK and embarked upon a truly wild journey. We re-learnt the skills of our primitive ancestors, including hunting, fishing and preparing the buckskin used to make our clothes. We foraged, crafted, preserved, pickled and dried, practised making fire and sculpted tools from rocks and bones. We had no phones, electricity, maps or sat nav, no chocolate or sugar, and no tent. We had only the food we foraged, the clothes we had made and the stars in the sky as our roof and our guide. Was it tough? Yes! Was it amazing? Completely! Would we do it again? Absolutely!

We came back from the trip both exhausted and revived. Living out in the wild with no modern equipment gave us a new perspective on life and we have some truly special stories of this primitive living experience that we now use to inspire both adults and children. We share some of these stories in this book.

Our passion is to connect people to their natural environment through skill acquisition and play. We believe that all children (and adults!) should be able to light a fire (safely) by the age of ten, know at least ten different uses for a stick and a stone, recognize at least five of the plants and trees they see daily, and be able to identify at least ten different birds that visit their back gardens. It is our mission, through this book, to enable them to do that.

Forest School Adventure is full of clear, step-by-step instructions to guide you and your children through nature awareness, bushcraft, primitive skills and wild food activities. Younger children can enjoy the simpler exercises with their parents and older children can discover new skills on their own. It can be used as a guide book for helping to identify plants and learning what to eat from nature's larder, a recipe book for making yummy food or it can be used for inspiring Forest School leaders and parents in ways to engage young people with their natural world.

The importance of play in nature

Increasingly, I look back to compare my childhood to the way things are for children now. When I was young, when my sisters and I were bored, we would complain to our parents that we had 'nothing to do'. We had no smart phones or computers then, but our parents knew something we would eventually discover – that outside there was a treasure trove of things to do. So their response was often, 'go outside and play'.

We would reluctantly drag ourselves out, complaining of being too tired to play, yet somehow we would entertain ourselves for hours. We would collect snails, build ramps, hunt for the hairiest caterpillars and dig for treasure (things I still do). When we finally came back in, we would be ravenously hungry, full of stories, enthusiastically planning future projects and completely re-energized. Dan talks of a similar scenario with his siblings. He had the freedom to roam around the green spaces close to his house, staying out until the sun went down or dinner was ready, whichever came first.

Abundant research confirms that interacting with nature nurtures children's creativity, promotes good health, raises vitamin levels, inspires problem-solving and builds confidence. I can support these findings through my own experiences working with children in nature and the fact that my oldest, deepest and most vivid memories are of moments spent outside playing. Now Dan and I watch our own children and their friends, occasionally bored, listless and uninspired inside, but finding a new passion for play once outside. Our six-year-old daughter has been sit spotting (see page 35), bug hunting

Some of the positive impacts of playing outside include:

- It promotes well-being and wholesome physical development.

- It can develop muscle strength and help with coordination.

- It can develop self-confidence and boosts creative thinking.

- It burns extra calories, which will help prevent obesity.

- It promotes good sleep and a healthy appetite.

- It exposes us to sunlight, which gives us a natural boost and makes us feel happier.

and den building since she could walk. She prides herself on her plant ID, fire lighting and whittling skills (with us by her side), and we're sure our one-year-old will follow suit.

Nature can be both a playground and a classroom, as well as a vast storehouse of things to eat and to build with. Some of a child's early encounters with nature are rites of passage: discovering the joys of stomping and splashing in puddles, building sandcastles, or releasing a cloud of fluffy parachutes by blowing on a dandelion seed head. With these discoveries come important, never-to-be-forgotten lessons, such as what happens when the muddy puddle is deeper than the height of your wellies, or what happens when you build that sandcastle too close to the tide line!

11

As children grow older, their interactions with nature become more complex and afford more learning opportunities: close encounters with a bramble bush allow them to experience the bliss of a ripe blackberry as well as the sharp prickle of thorns. The four-year-old who keeps a ladybird as a pet in an airtight matchbox may be inconsolable when she discovers it has died, but begins an understanding about loss, grief and habitat that will last a lifetime. And there's no need to convince someone of the value of identifying a dock leaf or plantain once they have been stung by a nettle. There are so many positive interactions with nature that could benefit both adults and children throughout their life if they are encouraged from a young age to be open to the journey.

Respecting nature

When you are enjoying activities outdoors, always remember the countryside code: respect, protect, enjoy.

- Respect other people. Consider the local community and other people enjoying the outdoors. Leave no trace of your visit and take your litter home.

- Leave gates and property as you find them. Farmers may have left gates open or closed to consider their livestock.

- Protect the natural environment. Help to conserve and preserve the natural environment by following paths unless wider access is available.

- Keep dogs under control. Think about sheep and cows. Your dog may be well behaved, but dogs can easily scare livestock.

- Enjoy the outdoors. Plan ahead and be prepared. Follow advice and local signs. Remember: take only photographs and leave only footprints.

Unfortunately, many of our green spaces have given way to houses and roads. Fear makes some parents unsure about letting their children roam too far. But nature doesn't always mean big woodlands or green parks. Nature can be in our back gardens or on our front doorsteps. We need to take the time to find it and allow ourselves to be free with our imaginations. Although the independence of roaming free is appealing to most children, interactions with nature can be just as fun shared with parents or older siblings. Our hope is that this book can act as a guide to allow these connections to take place.

Safety preparation

Throughout the book you will find safety guides and advice where necessary. Remember, proper **PREPARATION** prevents poor performance.

P = Precaution
Prepare your space beforehand. Do you have all the safety measures in place, such as water for fire extinguishing or heatproof gloves or tongs to take hot things off a fire or stove?

R = Research
Find out about your subject first, especially when foraging. Use field guides to help when you are out and about. Learning is part of the fun.

E = Environment
Understand and know your environment. Just because you are outside doesn't make the area safe. Look up, down and all around. Make sure you are safe.

P = Preparation
Make sure you have everything you need before you start. That way your activity will be conducted calmly and without any mistakes.

A = Awareness
Be aware of others around you, especially when using tools.

R = Respect
Make sure you are respectful of the environment you are in. Follow the rules and guidelines when out and about. These will help keep you safe and preserve the natural environment for other people.

A = Adult supervision
Make sure a responsible adult is supervising when working with tools or fire.

T = Take your time
Don't rush; it can cause mistakes. Take your time and enjoy yourself.

I = Injuries
Make sure you have a full first-aid kit with you at all times.

O = Order
Keep your tools and equipment in order. If you are planning to use tools, keep them sharp. A blunt tool can be a hazard.

N = Never guess
If you are not sure about something, ask.

Nature Awareness

DEVELOP A RELATIONSHIP WITH NATURE BY SHARPENING
UP YOUR SENSES. BE AWARE OF THE SMELL IN THE AIR JUST
BEFORE A RAINSTORM. SIT SILENTLY UNDER A TREE AND
OBSERVE NATURE GO ABOUT HER DAILY ROUTINE AROUND
YOU. TASTE A FRESH, JUICY WILD BLACKBERRY. FEEL HOW
THE BARK OF AN OAK TREE FEELS AGAINST YOUR FINGERS.
OPEN YOURSELF UP TO NATURE AND SHE WILL SHOW YOU
A WHOLE MAGICAL WORLD OF ADVENTURE.

Nature crafts

Whatever the time of the year, nature has an amazing stationery cupboard available to us for craftmaking. There is an abundance of things you can use to sculpt, mould, stick, collage and make beautiful artwork. The beauty of most nature crafts is that they need few resources or planning and some go straight back into the earth to be recomposted. They can simply be left where they have been created, so when you have completed your art or craft activity, don't forget to take a photo, as just like the moving tide taking away a sandcastle, the wind or rain may reclaim your art.

Bird feeder

This is a great activity for the winter months when birds' food stores are depleting. They will appreciate extra help in getting their food so they can survive through this cold season.

AGE Any
TIME 10+ minutes
TOOLS Garden sack (optional), scissors
MATERIALS Lard, bird seed, pine cones, string, bowl. Plastic gloves and aprons are all advisable

Step 1
Gather as many pine cones as you want to make bird feeders. Mix together the lard and bird seed in a bowl and squish them together with your hands.

Step 2
Tie the string to the top of the pine cone, leaving a long tail to tie it onto a tree or bird-feeding station.

Step 3
Squash the mixture around the pine cone, making sure it sinks into all the nooks and crannies of the cone.

Step 4
Tie the cone to a tree and wait patiently until the birds begin to trust their gift from you.

Tip
It is possible to make a feeder without pine cones, but if you use a pine cone as a base the lard sticks better to its form and the bird feeder will hold together for longer.

1

2

3

4

Bug hotel

Of all the animal species on Earth, an estimated nine out of ten of them are insects. Some can bite, sting and even spread germs. But don't let that scare you: only a few kinds of insects do us any harm. Most insects are good guys! They clean up; they add goodness to our soil to help food grow; some help pollinate flowers to help grow delicious fruits; others fight the bad bugs. It is our job to look after them and make them feel welcome in our gardens. Try making a bug hotel to encourage them to stay.

AGE 4+
TIME 20 minutes
TOOLS Scissors, can opener (if using a tin can)
MATERIALS Recycled plastic bottle (or empty tin can, see box), pen, length of string or garden twine approx. 2ft (60cm), small twig about ½in (1cm) in diameter and 2in (5cm) long, sticks, twigs, seed heads, pine cones, wood shavings, lichen

Step 1
With the help of an adult, cut the top and the bottom off the plastic bottle with scissors so that you are left with a tube shape.

Step 2
Pierce a hole in the middle of the tube, using a pen or scissors, and another hole underneath on the opposite side.

Step 3
Thread the length of string through both holes. Pull it through, leaving a tail of about 3in (7.5cm). Tie this tail around the small twig. This will prevent the string from pulling all the way through. Leave enough string at the opposite end to be able to tie a loop to hang the bug hotel up.

Step 4
Gather up some natural materials for filling the plastic tube: sticks, twigs, moss, pine cones, dried leaves etc.

Step 5
Fill the bottle with the bug-loving materials you have collected. Make sure everything is tightly packed together with tiny crevices for your bugs to hide in. Hang it up in your garden using the loop of string and leave for the bugs to find their way in.

Variations
You can also use a clean, empty tin can. Using a can opener, take off the opposite end, making it into a hollow tube. Fill with your collected materials and hang up using string tied around the outside.

You can make tiny bug hotels, too, by collecting handfuls of dried leaves and wrapping them in a large bunch of twigs. Wrap jute string around the outside and tie in a tight knot. Leave a long tail to tie the can onto fences and trees and watch as the bugs check in.

1

2

Tip
This is a great way to recycle plastic bottles or tin cans. Two good deeds in one activity! It has to be a winner.

3

4

5

PLAYING WITH CLAY

Clay is nature's answer to play dough. There is so much messy fun to be had with a ball of clay; grab a ball and then simply let your imagination run wild.

Exploring the process of using naturally sourced clay from start to finish is a great way to understand more about its qualities and unpredictable characteristics. See step 1 of 'Processing natural clay' on page 125 for information on how to source natural clay. However, if you prefer, you can find air-dry clay in craft shops or online at various retailers.

Trolls, elves and goblins

This is one of my favourite activities with clay. I've seen people of all ages enjoying this. I love watching balls of clay get transformed into amazing characters.

Roll a small ball of clay for the head and a larger ball for the body. Insert a small stick into the head, leaving the end of it poking out to attach the body onto. This is a good way to help the two pieces stay together as the piece dries.

Insert two small sticks into the body, to make the legs. Try making it look as if the goblin is sitting on his clay bottom with his legs out in front of him to avoid putting pressure on his stick legs.

Now use your imagination with whatever natural materials are to hand: add seed eyes, moss hair, a leaf beard and whatever else your troll desires.

Leave the clay to dry somewhere out of the elements. If it gets wet again your troll will return to wet clay.

Hedgehogs

These little fellows look great guarding a woodpile, in a fireplace or on a doorstep. Just make sure they are protected from the rain!

Make your hedgehog body and head from one piece of clay. Give him an oval body with a pointy head. Now cover him in tiny sticks for his prickles, and add four sticks at the bottom to make his legs. Leave the clay to dry somewhere safe and dry out of the elements.

Clay bugs

It is best to use air-dry clay for this to save disappointment as it dries. Don't leave it out afterwards, as the rain will turn it back into sloppy clay.

Grab a ball of clay. Decide what bug to make. It could be one that exists only in your imagination that has ten wings, six eyes and a beard! Press leaves in to make wings; push sticks in to make legs and antennae; find acorn shells or seeds to make eyes, and so on. Leave the clay to dry somewhere safe and dry out of the elements.

Clay tree spirits

I believe all trees have a spirit trapped inside them. Some are obvious, with their knots and bark creating surprised expressions and their branches reaching up like arms; others need encouragement and imagination to release their characters.

Find an interesting tree. It could be big or small, old or young, thick or thin. Press a big dollop of clay (or sticky mud) onto the tree. This will be the tree's face. Use this as a base into which you can mould or press natural materials to create features. Give your tree a moustache from long grasses, beady eyes with acorn shells, hair with moss, and so on. You could even use your clay like glue to stick on arms with twigs.

Leaf and flower plaques

These clay plaques are lovely hung up to bring a bit of nature inside your home. Experiment with the flowers and foliage you can find outside. You could even paint them afterwards as a colourful alternative.

AGE 3+
TIME 5+ minutes
TOOLS Rolling pin
MATERIALS Air-dry clay, leaves, flowers and sticks

Step 1
You will need a small collection of plants, leaves and flowers, but make sure you know what you are picking. If you are not 100% sure you can identify it, leave it. I've found that common weeds and plants, such as daisies, dandelions, plantain, ivy and hawthorn leaves, are lovely for this. You don't need much, so only pick a few of each thing.

Step 2
Roll out a fist-sized piece of clay to make a tile shape, about ³⁄₈in (1cm) thick.

Step 3
Place your chosen leaves and flowers onto the clay tile. Use the rolling pin to roll gently over the plants. Do this a few times to ensure their pattern has transferred onto the clay.

Step 4
Now take away the plants. You should be left with a beautiful indent.

Step 5
You can leave the plaque natural or paint it in bright colours so that your design pops out.

Tip
Use a stick to make two holes at the top to hang the plaque up with string. Make sure it is at least ³⁄₈in (1cm) thick where you make them so it is strong enough to hold the weight.

1

2

3a

3b

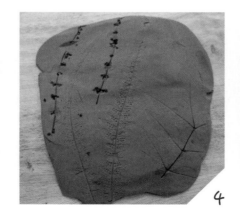
4

5

NATURAL COLLAGES AND SCULPTURES

Nature provides us with wonderful materials to make art with: stunning colours, shapes, textures and sizes. You can use these materials to make some creative art. Your imagination is the only limit. The beauty of these pieces of natural artwork is that they are temporary and will be returned back to nature, sometimes even within hours! It is always a good idea to take a photo as a reminder.

Look around you before you decide what to make. Sometimes the materials will guide you and show you what is possible. Decide whether you want to make a 3D structure that stands proud and tall or a framed picture that sits beautifully on the ground.

Gather your materials. It is a good idea to only use what is abundant or already on the ground. Remember: if in doubt, leave it out!

Create a wonderful picture or sculpture by placing or building up your materials.

Use clay or mud as a natural glue for sticking, and charcoal for drawing.

Ideas for sculptures
- Make an abstract piece of art. Art does not always have to look like something we recognize; sometimes it is about making something interesting, beautiful or thought-provoking.

- Make a 3D person – maybe a self-portrait?

- Make a 3D creature – a centipede from a log with a hundred sticks for legs; a snail made from a nest of grass; a bird made with logs, feathers and stones, etc.

Ideas for natural collages

• Use the seasons as a guide. Divide your picture into four sections. Think about what you might see or feel during each season and use natural materials to represent this: bright dandelions in summer representing the sun, brown leaves representing autumn, a snowman made from daisies and such like.

• Use natural materials to create a favourite holiday memory, as if your picture were a photograph on the ground.

• Create a picture of yourself or a friend.

3D maps

This can be used as a craft activity or as part of a fun game. It's great for encouraging creativity, getting to know the area you are in and understanding the features of the surrounding environment.

AGE 3+
TIME 10+ minutes
TOOLS None
MATERIALS
Whatever can be found on the ground: stones, twigs, leaves etc.

As a group, or individually, walk around the area you are in. Notice the big features and the small. Are there any trees that particularly stand out? Is there a hedge line? Is there a difference in size in the trees and plants? Is there a stream, a path, a gate, maybe? Take note of these things.

Decide on names for the features that stick out: 'the wise old oak tree'; 'the wiggly jiggly path'; 'the happy family of trees', and so on.

Mark out an area about 3 x 3ft (1 x 1m) using logs. Use the natural materials that are around to create a 3D map of the area within this log frame. Once it is finished, share with others, talking them through the map and explaining the key features.

3D map game
To play this as a game, you will need two or more players. Each person will make their own map but not talk anyone through its features when they have finished. One player will hide a clothes peg somewhere in the surrounding area without the other player(s) seeing. He or she will then come back and place a peg in the corresponding area of the map. The other player(s) then have to find the hidden peg based on its location on the map, trying to decipher what all the sticks, stones, pine cones and so on, symbolize.

Goblin village and mini dens

I always start this activity with a story about how you don't see goblins around any longer, because their village was destroyed by a dragon (see box below). After hearing it, the children suggest that we could rebuild the village – theme park, gardens and bridges galore!

AGE 3–6 years
TIME 15+ minutes
TOOLS None
MATERIALS Natural materials such as moss, sticks, leaves and stones

Decide what to build. A post office, a house, a park? Find areas of the wood that have interesting characteristics: a hole at the bottom of a tree, creeping roots, low overhanging branches, and such like.

Use natural materials to create tiny dens. Add leaves on sticks for miniature trees, pebbles lined up as bridges, moss for roofs and more. You can use small teddies or other toys as a guide for size.

The story of the goblin village (for inspiration)

This is my story about goblins, but you can tell your own to create any adventure you like!

'Have you ever seen a goblin? No? Well, that's because they no longer come here. Believe it or not, but here, where we stand, there used to be the most awesome goblin village. It had houses that were joined by epic bridges and gardens that looked like theme parks. It had cinemas, sweet shops and dance halls where goblins would come together at the end of every day for a good old boogie! But then one day, a dragon, a very friendly but really quite big dragon, who lived all the way up the hill, heard about these dances. He loved to dance, and desperately wanted to join in the fun.

'So, on one particularly rainy day, he put on his dancing shoes and ran down from the top of the valley to find the dance hall. But the rain had turned the ground into a muddy, sloppy mess, and the dragon's shoes were meant only for dancing, not for running, so he slipped all the way down. He slipped past all the trees, through the forest, down the hill and landed in a heap, squashing the whole village. Not a building was left standing. The goblins had no choice to move on, and now no one knows where they live. It's terribly sad. I wish there was some way we could help....'

Nest building

Have you seen how birds build their nests? Isn't it clever? With no teaching, they instinctively know how to build a nest using just their beaks! Could you do that? Try using some of the materials they do to weave a solid nest. Use grasses, bits of fluff, sticks, feathers, leaves, mud and more.

AGE Any
TIME 10+ minutes
TOOLS None
MATERIALS Any natural materials you can find, e.g. grass, sticks, feathers, mud

To begin, take a rough bundle of grass, make a loop and then weave in the ends to create your nest-like shape. Start small and keep adding materials, threading more materials in, weaving long grasses through. Then just keep adding. See how long it takes you to get something that resembles a bird's nest. It might be harder than you think!

Storytelling stones

I love a good story, fiction or fact, but if you're anything like me, your brain may go blank if someone asks you to tell one. Therefore, I made myself some story stones so I could have a new tale to tell any time, any place. Get creative when making your own and you'll be amazed at the elaborate tales you can weave.

AGE Any
TIME 20+ minutes
TOOLS
Chalkboard pens
MATERIALS Flat
stones to draw on

Find some stones. Beaches are a good place, but garden centres often sell bags of stones. The stones should be around 1 x 1in (2.5 x 2.5cm) to be able to fit a good picture on them.

Draw pictures on one side of your stones – people, animals, types of weather, numbers, symbols, or anything else you can think of. Once you have at least ten stones designed use them to tell stories around the campfire. Nominate one person as 'the storyteller'. Everyone chooses a story stone and gives it to the storyteller who has a minute to think about a story and share it with everyone else.

Ideas for using the stones
Make different sets of stones. Have a set that is just people, just animals, just symbols, or just weather conditions, and then choose a stone from each set for the story.

You can ask other people to choose a number of stones depending on the time available: if you only have five minutes, maybe just choose three; if you have half an hour, pick more.

Leaf printing

As a child, I loved making bark rubbings using crayons so the bark pattern of a tree transferred onto paper. Now I'm older I still love bark rubbing; our daughter does too, using her designs to make wrapping paper. I've also discovered this is a great way to transfer the patterns and colours of nature's plants.

AGE Any
TIME 5+ minutes
TOOLS Chopping board (or any hard surface), scissors, hammer, mallet or pounding stone
MATERIALS Cotton sheet, common abundant plants

Step 1
Cut out a square from the cotton sheet to the size you desire.

Step 2
Collect various plants you wish to use in your design. Bracken, buttercups, dock leaves and tree leaves all work well. Be sure you don't pick anything poisonous – remember, if in doubt, leave it out. Only use fresh plants and flowers and only pick from areas where the plants are abundant.

Step 3
Place your leaves and plants either one at a time or arranged in a pattern on the chopping board or hard surface. Place the cotton square over the top. Using the hammer or mallet, repeatedly hit the area with your plants underneath and watch as your colourful pattern comes through!

Tip
This activity works best in spring and summer when the leaves and plants are full of moisture.

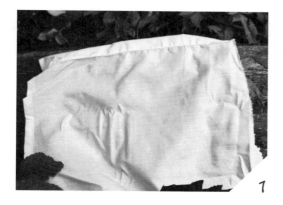

1

2

3

Variations

Use these beautiful pieces of art as part of another project. Tie them onto a stick to make a wall hanging or tapestry, or sew a few of them together to make a nature collector's bag.

Skills and learning

Nature has so much to offer us; sometimes all we need is a little imagination and a whole new world of activities opens up to us. I find everywhere you look in nature there is learning to be had. Under every log there is a creature teaching us a new way of life. We only need to look to the creatures of the forest to learn about being masters of camouflage, to the sky to learn about peripheral vision or observe our night watch nocturnal friends to learn about epic night vision. Nature has so much to offer us; it's just about knowing where to look. We can use our powers of observation to find out more about nature, or our detective skills to discover the hidden life of the forest.

Mini beast hunting

AGE Any
TIME 5+ minutes
TOOLS None
MATERIALS
Collecting pots, magnifying glass

There's a tiny world out there that most of us know nothing about – a world where the bugs and beasts of the underground and overground go about their everyday chores; finding food, storing food, finding cover and mostly concentrating on not getting eaten by something bigger. Why not go on a hunt to find some of these creepy-crawlies?

Think where you would hide if you were a bug, trying to hide away or have a sleep. Look in the nooks and crannies of trees, under logs and in hedges. Where would you go if you were a slug or snail and wanted to find a cold, dark, damp place to chill out? If you have a magnifying glass you can get up close, but it's amazing what our naked eyes can see, too, when we really look hard. Make sure you put all the bugs back where you found them.

Night vision

Did you know that we can actually see in the dark without any high-tech equipment? I remember using this technique for the first time and being astonished at how well it worked. I had been sitting around a campfire and decided it was time for bed. My tent was some way through the forest, and it was pitch black. I was taught this technique and surprisingly found my way back to my tent, navigating over rocks, avoiding logs and weaving around trees arriving at my tent safe and sound.

AGE 5+
TIME 15+ minutes
TOOLS None
MATERIALS A campfire at night

I urge you to try this simple technique next time you find yourself in the dark around the fire. It is a great way to retrain your night-vision abilities.

Firstly, it's a waiting game. Unless it's total darkness around you, it won't work. Spend the time while it is light making a fire and collecting wood to keep it going. Once it is dark, cover one eye with a hand or close one eye. If you're anything like me, however, it's really hard not to peek halfway through, so wearing an eye patch is handy and a great excuse to look like a pirate.

With your open eye, stare into the fire for 15 minutes. Chat to your friend, look for faces in the fire – anything to distract you from the time – but do not look away.

When the 15 minutes is up, look away from the fire and cover the eye that has been open, while opening up the eye that has been closed. Stare into the darkness. You'll be amazed at how clearly you can see, even with just one eye. It's suddenly like you're wearing invisible night-vision glasses. It certainly doesn't last forever, but long enough to experience natural night vision.

Muddy tracks

Tracking can mean many different things. To me, it is about being a detective, searching for clues, taking in evidence and making a story of what happened. Who was here? What did they do? What happened? You could find a footprint, a hoof mark or claw marks. You could find scattered feathers, a collection of nutshells, a bit of fur or blood or even bones. We may never know if our theory is correct, but part of the joy of tracking is in creating a story. Here is a simple way of developing your tracking skills and improving your observation.

Tip
Sand works well to begin with as you can clearly see tracks in it. You can move on to mud once you develop your tracking skills.

AGE 5+
GROUP SIZE 2+
TIME 5+ minutes
TOOLS None
MATERIALS Mud or sand, long sticks for the edges of the pit

Step 1

Create a pit at least 3 x 2ft (90 x 60cm) by laying out sticks to form the edges. The bigger the pit the better the tracks will be. Fill the pit with mud or sand (see box). This is your tracking pit. Working one at a time in pairs or small groups, one person will decide how to move through the tracking pit. They could run, hop or jump; move slowly or quickly; heavy-footed or light.

Step 2

While the other partner or rest of the group aren't looking, the person will move through the tracking pit in his or her chosen style. Now the others must decipher how it was done by looking at the tracks made. Look closely at the depth and width of track. Did the sand move anywhere else? Come up with an answer and ask the track maker. Discuss the results.

1

2

Story tracks

In small groups (a minimum of three groups works best), collect items from around you, such as a phone, keys, clothes, tools, food, etc. Decide on a simple story. Make tracks in your pit to fit your scenario and scatter the items around the pit. Now ask a new group to come in and work out what happened here. Who was here? How fast or slow were they moving? Behave like detectives and try to figure out each scenario. It's interesting to hear what different stories the groups come up with!

Sit spot

These days, the idea of spending ten minutes in a woodland, meadow or garden, sitting quietly and soaking up the atmosphere, is close to my idea of heaven. This is what we call a 'sit spot'. For toddlers, teenagers and fully fledged grown-ups, a sit spot is a great activity. Yes, it's a great excuse to be pardoned from chores, housework or homework, but it is also an opportunity to have a special experience and develop a connection to nature.

AGE Any
TIME Any
TOOLS None
MATERIALS None

Everybody finds a tree and just takes the time to sit for between 5–20 minutes before gathering together. Sit spots are a way of providing space to take time to be still and observe nature. How long you sit for is not important as long as it's done with a sense of importance. It's a good idea to choose the same spot each time to give you a chance to get to know your spot so you notice changes, new tracks and observe the habits of the creatures that share your area with you. Your special spot could even be at the bottom of your garden or on your front door step.

All you have to do is choose a quiet spot, put your peripheral vision into practice and try to be still. There's a whole other world out there that many of us know little about and a sit spot can be the perfect way to allow a spark of curiosity into nature's countless mysteries. See page 36 for a special sit spot story.

Things to look and listen for

- What plants are there
- Spiders weaving webs
- Birdsong, bird alarm calls and other noises
- Squirrels burying or digging for nuts
- Animal tracks
- Animal's fur transferred onto twigs
- Bark rubbed off trees, indicating deer rubbing their antlers
- Birds collecting materials for nests
- Ants doing busy 'collecting work'

NATURE AWARENESS

Sit spot stillness

ON MY WAY TO MY SIT SPOT, I STOP OFF AT THE SMALL POND TO COLLECT SOME CATTAIL DOWN AND FIND A FOX WHO HAS GIVEN HERSELF BACK TO THE EARTH. THE CATTAILS ARE NOT YET TALL ENOUGH; I WILL WAIT A FEW MONTHS BEFORE HARVESTING THEM TO WEAVE INTO A MAT. I GIVE THANKS TO THE FOX AS I COLLECT SOME RIB BONES, WHICH I WILL TURN INTO NEEDLES FOR SEWING. I AM FOREVER GRATEFUL FOR THE OFFERINGS OF NATURE.

The nettles have grown to about waist height. I forage some fresh tips to make pesto later. The trees are in full canopy now. The vivid scent of the woods on a humid day takes me back to my childhood. I approach my sit spot as quietly as I can, trying to let my body take

> *"I approach my sit spot as quietly as I can, trying to let my body take over from my mind."*

over from my mind. I attempt to adapt my clumsy human movements to mimic the delicate footstep of a deer, the gentle pad of a fox. The birds are not fooled by my awkward steps, cracking sticks beneath my lumbering feet, snagging my clothes on brambles. The birds set off a low-level domino-effect warning of my presence throughout the woodlands and scatter from the trees. I feel like I am a giant in the beating heart of the woods.

I reach my spot, take a deep breath and relax, slowly melting into the woods. I want to blend in and become invisible. I open my eyes wide like an owl. A treecreeper visits, letting out high-pitched chattering while dancing up and down a hazel tree looking for bugs. The usual song of the birds is broken. I sense the change in song whisper through the woodlands before a deathly silence. Flying fast past my eyes comes a hungry female sparrowhawk, looking to prey on unsuspecting birds. She does not succeed this time. I hear a buzzard call in the distance. A robin comes to see if I have anything to offer. A spider weaves her web. I have been at my sit spot for about an hour and slowly make my way home.

My sit spot chose me one day when I went for a wonder through the woods. I was standing at the base of a mighty oak tree. Its thick, above-ground roots offered me a seat and I accepted. Before I knew it, three hours had passed! This was my spot.

> *"My sit spot chose me one day when I went for a wonder through the woods."*

When I first found these woods, they were just starting to show me some of their magic. The woods were still bare from winter. I remember thinking how incredible it was that you could see deep into the heart of this living place, like looking through a keyhole into a secret world. Then the ramsons started to appear, first like a thick green blanket, then a wash of white flowers carpeting the woodland floor and scenting the air with a hint of garlic. Each season, these woods are like a new place. From my sit spot I watch the seasons change.

In summer, the canopy envelopes everything, capturing all the sun's rays except a few beams that puncture the roof of the woods and burst dappled shafts of light onto the forest floor. The animals are playful and relaxed as food is more abundant. The sweet scents of wildflowers drift through on the gentle breeze.

With autumn come berries, providing a sweet feast for the birds. The deer slowly change their light summer coats to more rugged winter hides. The squirrels store hazelnuts and acorns underground. Trees change the colour of their leaves as they collect the last of the sun's energy before a long hibernation. Everything is giving a final big push to head into the darkest times. In winter the woods bare all, revealing their secrets. The birds are quieter, the days are short, and the nights are long and cold.

I try to visit my sit spot every day, even if just for five minutes. My sit spot lets me see into a world that most people sadly don't get to. I have learned the language of the birds: their companion calls, their alarm calls and their beautiful thanksgiving songs at dawn. I have sat and watched a spider build its web, watched ants marching up and down trees collecting food, heard the tawny owl call out at night, observed a mouse panicking as he tried to conceal his larder of nuts, and had a squirrel jump over my legs.

"I have learned the language of the birds: their companion calls, their alarm calls and their beautiful thanksgiving songs at dawn."

After every sit spot I write down what I saw and share my stories with others, even if seemingly 'nothing' happened. The natural world is magical. We can all visit it when we allow the time to be still, becoming part of it, letting nature carry on as if we were not there. There is a whole other world out there that many of us know little about. A sit spot can be the perfect way to allow a spark of curiosity into some of nature's countless mysteries.

STALKING WALKS

Stalking walks are a great way to get a group ready for the day. Imitating these animals will give an insight into how they walk or fly, look, listen and stalk. These activities can be enjoyed by individuals, too. They are great for developing and sharpening your senses (such as sight and hearing) and improving your stealth skills.

Owl eyes

Owls are known for their fantastic vision, but did you know that humans have great eyesight, too? Our eyes evolved to see movement, and when we use our vision we can see from in front of our face to just in front of our ears!

Stand in an area where there is enough space for everybody taking part to stretch out their arms. Stretch them in front of your body and wiggle your fingers. Looking forwards, slowly move your hands out to the sides until they are just out of vision. This should be somewhere in line with your ears.

Stretch out your arms again and, looking forwards, move them up and down until they just go out of sight. You will be amazed at how much you can see. The more you practise with your owl eyes (your peripheral vision), the better you will be at spotting movement – just like a great hunter.

Fox walk

Foxes are sneaky scavengers and can move very silently and slowly. This exercise helps you find your inner fox.

Stand in an area where there is enough space for everybody taking part to spread out and stand still.

Try taking one single step that takes 30 seconds to complete. This is the part of the step where your leg takes a stride. Move it forwards as slowly and smoothly as you can.

Now practise placing your foot down stealthily: heel down first, then the outside of the foot, then place the whole foot down.

Combine the 30-second step with the stealth foot and get the group to move through the open area, going very, very slowly.

Deer listen and leap

Deer have a great sense of smell and really amazing hearing; their big, alert ears are always listening out for danger.

To listen like a deer, be completely silent. Once you have heard all the different sounds around you, cup your hands behind your ears. Listen again, and your hearing should be amplified. Now you are hearing like deer, leap and jump around like deer, too.

Flour trail tracker

This is a great exercise that evokes lots of imagination. We usually set one team to be the hunters and the other to be a mammoth. The hunters dress up with camouflage paint on their faces to create a really exciting atmosphere. This activity encourages children to use their observation skills and tune into their senses as well as their environment, unleashing their inner cave man and woman.

Out hunting, a group of hunters manage to shoot a mammoth with a bow and arrow, but unfortunately only injure him. The mammoth escapes into the bush, leaving a trail of blood behind him. The hunters are now on a tight timeframe to locate the mammoth before he gets too far away.

AGE 6+
TIME 15+ minutes
TOOLS Walkie-talkie radios are desirable but not essential
MATERIALS Flour

Split those taking part into two teams. Name one group the mammoth and the other the hunters. Give each group walkie-talkies if you have them. Give the mammoth group two minutes to get away (depending on the size of the area and the boundaries set, you may want to vary the time allowance).

The mammoth group members must travel in a line, one behind the other. The person at the front sprinkles a handful of flour as the group walks along to symbolize the blood trail. The flour can also be used to mark arrows splashed onto trees. These can be subtle or relatively obvious depending on the age and ability of the group. Once the front person has left a mark, he or she goes to the back and lets the next one in line leave a mark, indicating the direction in which they are travelling. Once the two minutes are up and they have run out of time, all the mammoth group will need to find somewhere to hide.

After two minutes, the hunters begin their hunt. If walkie-talkies are being used, they can communicate that they have left and the groups can send gruesome noises to one another over the airwaves. The hunters can then follow the flour trail to find their prey. Again, they must travel in a line, one behind the other. The person at the front is the only one looking for a sign. When the front person has found a mark, he or she then goes to the back and so on until the mammoth is found.

Observation stations

This is a great activity for those wanting to test their powers of observation. It challenges your sense of sight and helps strengthen your field of vision.

Using the string, mark out an area in one long line. This is what the participants stand behind and marks the length of your area. Place the items within your chosen area, reaching out about a maximum of 20 large paces away from your string. Use all of the area. Put some of the items up close and others far away. Loop some of the items over branches, and lean big items up against trees. Match the colour or shape of your items to blend into the natural environment. Do not hide the items; make sure that you can still see them when you stand behind the string line. Don't tell the people who will be observing what you've hidden or how many items there are.

Bring your observers together to stand behind the string and tell them that they must try to spot as many 'foreign' items as they can. They must remain quiet throughout and not signal to others when they spot something. Test them afterwards and see how many things they spotted.

AGE 5+
TIME 10+ minutes
TOOLS None
MATERIALS Ten or so items of varying sizes and colours, length of string/cord

Variations
Instead of having the observers stand behind a line, hide the items in an area of woodland, placing them on both the right- and left-hand sides of the path they are to follow. Get the observers to move silently through this area and see how many items they can spot without stopping.

GET TO KNOW A TREE

There are many ways in which you can get to know a tree. Feel its bark, stand back and admire it, if possible find out its history and work out its height and age. Below are some ways you can do that – and no, you don't have to chop down a tree to guess its age!

Touch the tree

Divide the group into pairs, in which one member will be blindfolded. The other will lead him or her safely to a tree (guiding by an elbow is advisable). At the tree, the person will be guided to feel the tree. Notice where its branches are. Is the bark rough or smooth? Is it a tall tree or stumpy? Does it have leaves that you can touch?

When the person has had enough time and is happy to do so, they should be led back (by a different way) to the place they started from to take off their blindfold. They then have to guess which tree was theirs. Then swap.

VARIATIONS For children aged 8+: with someone helping to guide them, get them to find their way back to the tree blindfolded.

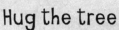

Hug the tree

This is a way to estimate the tree's age without chopping it down to count its rings. This will be a rough estimate! Each tree grows at a different rate, so there is no foolproof method that works for all trees. Also, we use our hand width as a guide and, just like trees, we are all different and therefore have different sizes of hands. But try this as a rough guide. Every tree enjoys a good hug, after all.

Each hand span equals about five years. See how many hand spans are needed to reach around the trunk of a tree. Add these up in multiples of five to see how old the tree is. It's fun to get a group of people involved and see how many people are needed to give the tree a group hug!

Look at the tree

Learn how to estimate a tree's height without a ruler! Stand with your back touching the tree you want to measure. Take a few giant steps away from the tree. Now put your head between your legs to look behind you. Can you see the top of the tree through your legs? If not, stand up and take a few more giant steps away. Keep checking the view in between your legs. When you can see the tip of the tree, count your paces back. Each pace should be around 3ft (1m) long. Therefore, if you can measure 20 paces back to the tree, your tree is approximately 65ft (20m) tall.

Camouflage hands

Whenever I teach camouflage skills, the first question I ask is: 'Is bright pink a camouflage colour?' to which I mostly receive a resounding 'No!'. But then, as they look at what the word actually means, people realize that pink actually could be a camouflage colour – if, for some reason, you needed to hide out in a field of the pinkest roses!

AGE Any
TIME 5+ minutes
TOOLS None
MATERIALS Natural materials such as leaves, mud and moss, water for making mud

Camouflage is the art of blending in to your natural environment and animals are the masters at it. Deer, with their many shades of brown, match the foliage and trees around them. Frogs, with their green skin, match the lily pads on ponds. Ducks blend into the rushes with their speckled feathers. Have you ever noticed that female animals often have more muted colours while males have more striking shades? Is this so the female can blend in to protect her young unnoticed while the male distracts predators, perhaps?

See how easy or hard it is to camouflage a part of your body. But remember: camouflage is not the art of hiding; it is the art of blending in.

Step 1

Choose a tree. Observe its colours, patterns, any knots, etc. Collect materials to match your tree's shades and textures. Make some mud using earth and water.

Step 2

Place your hand on your tree. Using the natural materials, decorate your hand to match the tree. Continue on to your arm for a more ambitious project.

Tip

For younger children, try using a stick and just camouflaging a finger.

1

2

Luminous camouflage

I WORK OUTDOORS ALL THE TIME AND IF I'M WORKING WITH GROUPS OF CHILDREN, I TEND TO WEAR BRIGHT COLOURS SUCH AS PINKS, REDS OR TURQUOISE, SO THAT I CAN BE LOCATED EASILY BY ANYONE WHO NEEDS ME. HOWEVER, IF I'M ON MY OWN, OR I'M VENTURING OUT FOR A SIT SPOT AND FANCY MY CHANCES OF SNEAKING UP ON SOME WILDLIFE, I WEAR MORE MUTED COLOURS THAT BLEND INTO THE NATURAL ENVIRONMENT: GREENS, BROWNS AND GREYS.

This was never more important than when I lived out in the wild. If I had any hope of creeping up on my dinner then I had to find ways to make myself invisible in the woods. Deer and squirrel would surely think me laughable for trying to act stealthily in pink! So I made my own clothes from leather. Natural and free! I felt 'quiet' walking through the

> "To an ordinary human being we probably smelled pretty bad, but to each other and to the wildlife, we smelled right!"

forest. I could literally step off the path a few paces ahead of my tribe and I would disappear from sight. Who better to impersonate in a grand game of hide and seek but the masters themselves, the stealth ninjas of the woods!

My clothes quickly picked up the smell and the shades of the surrounding environment. Walking through a burned forest, we turned black in both skin and clothes. Adventures in berry bushes

added rich purples. Patches of mossy green were taken from muddy woodland seats, with the underlining colours of the deer covering the rest of us. To an ordinary human being we probably smelled pretty bad, but to each other and to the wildlife, we smelled right! However, soon enough we realised that camouflage is only as effective as the environment you are in.

One day we discovered our path blocked due to a massive forest fire. Trees were still smouldering. The ground was burning our feet. Our path had gone, covered by deep, hot ash. We could no longer follow our desired route through the mountains. Up until then we had not seen another human being – or at least we'd made sure another human being did not see us. Any sight or sound of another human and we would leap like skittish animals into bushes.

So now we had a dilemma. We had two clear choices ahead of us. One: to keep walking and quite possibly never find a new path, thereby getter deeper and

deeper into the wilderness; or two: rejoin our path by taking a cut through a village deep down in the valley.

We decided that option two was probably the best way of assuring we didn't get lost forever in the wilderness. It took a good few hours, trekking further and further and following our noses towards civilisation. And there it was, suddenly: road signs, people, shops, tourists! This was more wild to us than the wilderness. In reality, it was actually a fairly small town, mostly blocked off from main roads, but it seemed epic to us and extraordinarily colourful and loud. Then we spied something that made us feel more at home: a berry-laden elder tree. Nature's sweet shop! We were delighted. We didn't waste time in picking the berries; we just chewed them straight from the tree's spindly branches like wild beasts, completely unaware of the staring eyes of the villagers.

A well-timed tourist bus cruised through at that exact moment. I'd love to have heard the commentary from the stunned tour guide! We went from being completely camouflaged to having giant alarms going off about our bodies. The clothes that had once made us invisible were now suddenly luminous, glowing brightly for all to stare at. We stuck out like a flock of flying pink sheep! Our teachers took the lead and walked on ahead to try and find the way to the other side where our path awaited us. The remaining four of us followed behind, wary of the 'strange people'. We felt like children lost in a big city.

Occasionally, our teachers would stop and talk to someone, humouring their curiosity. We only found out later that when asked who we were, our teachers had said that we four were their children who had lived out in the wild for the last 27 years and we'd only come down into this village to find us husbands and wives! Even more surprisingly, one woman apparently offered her son to become my husband but then remembered it wouldn't work as he lived in California.

It was a long hike that day, covering about 13 miles or so. That might not sound like a lot, but barefoot with a large pack and the weight of so many eyes, it felt like double. None of us minded: anything to get back to being our discreet wild selves.

"The clothes that had once made us invisible were now suddenly luminous, glowing brightly for all to stare at."

Bushcraft

BUSHCRAFT IS A WAY OF THRIVING IN THE NATURAL
ENVIRONMENT. IT IS ALL ABOUT LEARNING HOW TO ENJOY
AND MAKE USE OF THE WILD COUNTRYSIDE AROUND US.
BUSHCRAFT IS ABOUT DEVELOPING SKILLS THAT HELP YOU
ADAPT TO YOUR SURROUNDINGS – FROM COOKING ON
A CAMPFIRE TO MAKING DENS AND PRACTICAL CRAFTS
USING NATURAL MATERIALS.

Knots

Knowing how to tie a range of basic knots is a really useful bushcraft skill that will help you in all manner of tasks from assembling a shelter to making an emergency stretcher. Here we teach you some of the most useful knots.

Glossary of knot terms

Bight A bight of rope refers to a bend in the rope.

Quick release A quick release knot is where a bight of rope has been pulled through while tying the knot. This is a safety feature that allows the knot to be untied quickly.

Frapping turn If you make a lashing, a frapping turn can be used to make it tight. You wrap the rope around and around and then pull the rope tight before tying off.

Working end The end of the rope you are using to tie the knot.

Standing end The end of the rope that stays still whilst tying the knot.

Hitch Attaches a rope to something. There are different types but the most commonly used is a double half hitch.

Loop A loop is made when a rope forms a partial circle with the ends crossing each other.

Clove hitch

The clove hitch is useful for starting or finishing a lashing such as a square lashing.

Step 1
Pass the end of the rope around the pole.

Step 2
Cross over the standing end.

Step 3
Loop it back around the pole.

Step 4
Thread it back under itself and pull tight.

Double half hitch

More secure than a single hitch, this is mainly used for finishing and tying off.

Step 1
Form a loop around your object with the rope.

Step 2
Pass the working end up through the loop.

Step 3
Pull the working end tight against object. Take the working end under the standing rope and pass it back through the loop.

Step 4
Pull the knot tight.

Siberian hitch

The Siberian hitch is an excellent knot for making a ridge line for supporting a tent, but should not be trusted for bigger loads as it could slip. This knot can be tied with gloved hands in cold weather and, with its quick release, is easily undone.

Step 1
Pass the rope over your hand and around the back of the tree.

Step 2
Pass the working end under your hand and back over your fingers.

Step 3
Pass the working end over both ropes between your hand and the tree and back under.

Step 4
Tuck a bight (bend) between your fingers.

Step 5
Pull this bight through the loop.

Step 6
Tighten the quick release.

Step 7
Pull the knot to the tree.

Step 8
To release, pull the tail.

Timber hitch

The timber hitch knot is great for pulling a log or a stack of sticks. This knot locks when you apply pressure by pulling an object, but practically falls apart when you release the rope.

Step 1
Pass the rope around the log.

Step 2
Pass the working end over the standing end (the non-moving piece).

Step 3
Bring the working end up on the log.

Step 4
Loop the working end around itself once.

Step 5
Loop the working end around itself once more.

Step 6
Then a third time. The friction of the knot will hold it tight.

Tip
The timber hitch is especially good for putting up a tarpaulin shelter or hammock. You can attach one side to a tree and know that it is secure. It is particularly good as it is self-tightening and easy to undo.

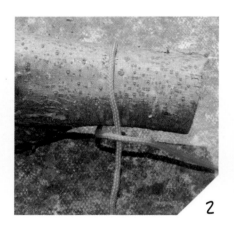

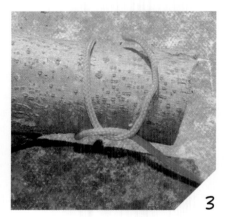

1 2 3 4 5 6

Sheet bend knot

This is a good knot to join two ropes together of different thicknesses. The thicker rope should be used for the bight (bend). It can also be used to join two ropes of the same thickness.

Step 1
Form a bight (bend) in one piece of rope.

Step 2
Pass the new piece of rope through the bight.

Step 3
Pass it around the back of the first piece of rope.

Step 4
To finish, tuck the new rope under itself and pull tight.

A quick-release knot
A sheet bend can be made as a quick-release knot – for example, when putting up a tarp on a tent line. Instead of passing the working end of the new rope under itself, pass a bight and pull tight.

1

2

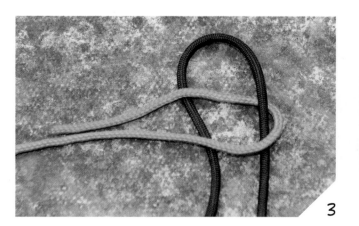

3

4

Prusik

The Prusik is a good knot for holding in place tarps on a tent line, as it locks in place under pressure. It is also easily moveable when pressure is released.

Step 1
Form a bight (bend) in the rope and place it over the tent line.

Step 2
Pull the two ends through the bight and wrap around tent line.

Step 3
Repeat step 2 and pull the knot tight.

Step 4
Attach the ends to your tarp loop and tie a sheet bend (see page 55) on a bight.

1

2

3

4

Tip
If putting up a larger tarp you can add in more loops around your tent line to make the Prusik stronger. Also with a large tarp, tie a sheet bend (see page 55) to attach to your tarp.

Slippery guy line knot

This knot is great for securing tarps and is adjustable under load. It can be undone under load, too. It is also known as a taut line.

Step 1
Bring the rope from your object (tarp) down around your peg to form a loop.

Step 2
Pass the working end through the loop and around the tight line.

Step 3
Repeat Step 2 twice. You will have three turns around the rope.

Step 4
Pass the working end behind the ropes leaving a bight of rope.

Step 5
Form a new bight of rope with the working end and pass it through the first bight to form the quick release.

Step 6
Tighten your knot and slide it upwards to tighten and downwards to release the pressure.

Canadian jam knot

This knot is useful for wrapping up and tying down sleeping bags and big loads, and uses little rope.
It is also known as an arbor knot.

Step 1
Form a loop in the rope.

Step 2
Pass the working end behind and through the loop to form an overhand knot.

Step 3
Follow Steps 1 and 2 to tie a second overhand knot next to the first.

Step 4
Pass the standing end of the rope around your object and through the first overhand knot.

Step 5
Pull the knots tight against your object.

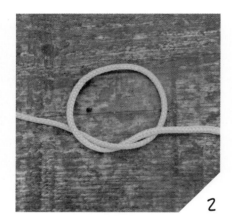

Square lashing

This knot is used to secure poles into a rectangle that can be used for a raft, tabletop and many other bushcraft items.

Step 1
Start by tying a clove hitch (see page 51) on the pole underneath, next to where the two poles form a cross.

Step 2
Wrap the working end over and under the poles alternating either side of the pole underneath. Do this three times, pulling tight as you go.

Step 3
When the wrapping has been done, bring the working end back around between the two logs and wrap three times round, pulling tight as you go. This is called a frapping turn (see page 50).

Step 4
With the working end, tie another clove hitch to finish.

Sledge knot

The sledge knot is a great alternative to tying a square lashing as it uses far less rope and is just as strong. Unlike the square lashing, it cannot be undone. We like to use this knot with a lean-to shelter, tying the cross bar to the trees.

Step 1
Wrap the rope twice around the pieces you want to bind together.

Step 2
Cross the rope over the standing end to form a cross.

Step 3
Form a loop over the standing rope.

Step 4
Wrap the working end around both ropes three times.

Step 5
Bring the working end up between the ropes. Tuck it under the first and second wraps.

Step 6
Bring the working end down through the loop and tighten. Slide up to the poles and pull tight.

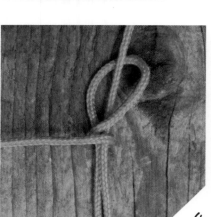

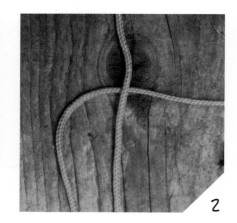

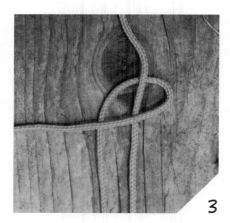

Hanking cord

This keeps all your cords nice and neat, ready to pick up and use next time.
When you need to use them again, just pull the end in the middle of the cord.

Step 1
Place the cord between your little finger and ring finger.

Step 2
Bring the working end around the back of your thumb.

Step 3
Cross over the cord and around your little finger to form a figure 8.

Step 4
Continue to do this until you have about 12in (30cm) of cord left.

Step 5
Pinch the middle of the cord where it crosses. Remove from hand and wrap the working end around the middle.

Step 6
Tie a clove hitch (see page 51) to finish.

1

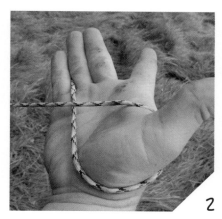
2

3

4

5

6

Shelters and dens

One of my favourite and completely free things to do is to build a shelter or base out of natural materials. The best place for this is in the woods. There you can find most of the materials you will need to construct your den, and there is often no need to cut anything down. We have also included some shelters that use tarps for a really quick and simple build. Of course, you can freestyle your own, but over the following pages are some simple designs to create some really great shelters.

A-frame

This simple shelter is fun to build for all ages and makes a great team-building challenge. See which team can make the best waterproof A-frame shelter. To make sure it is truly waterproof, test it with a full watering can afterwards!

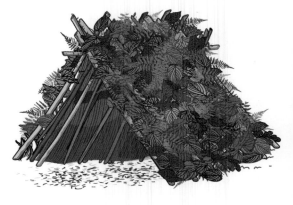

AGE 4+
TIME 45+ minutes
TOOLS Folding saw, leaf litter bag (optional)
MATERIALS Leaves, wood, grasses, string/paracord
KNOTS Canadian jam knot (see page 58)

Step 1
Find a log that is as tall as you with your arm stretched above your head, and two large sticks with forked ends that reach the tallest person's chest. These will be used to make the doorway to your shelter.

Step 2
Make the log and sticks into a triangular shape, leaning the forked sticks inwards towards one another so that they link and hold together. If you want to guarantee that it will hold, you can tie them together with paracord using a Canadian jam knot. Now place your ridge pole on top of your triangle. You can tie these all together if you like with another jam knot or some square lashing. These should form a sturdy base for your shelter.

Step 3
Cover both sides with twigs and sticks, making sure to keep enough space inside for a person to lie down. Children often think of this like creating a rib cage. Each stick should have a place; smaller ones down at the bottom, longer ones towards the doorway, like completing a big 3D shelter puzzle. Make sure you leave the doorway free of sticks so that you can get inside, though!

Step 4
Start covering the frame from the ground up, using leaves, twiggy branches and grass. For a well-insulated, waterproof layer you need a thickness of about fingertip to elbow in depth. If you are planning to stay out in your shelter overnight, add a thin all-over covering, and maybe throw a tarp over the top in case of rain.

Baker's tarp

A tarp is a simple and quick way to make a shelter that doesn't destroy the local mini-beasts' habitats. There are many tarps designed for camping; we use one with 19 points, which can give you many configurations for shelters. We offer two different designs of tarp shelters over the next few pages. The baker's tarp shelter is great for groups to sleep under on long, summer nights.

AGE 4+
TIME 10+ minutes
TOOLS Mallet
MATERIALS Tarp 10 x 10ft (3 x 3m), enough rope/cord to fit between two trees (about 30ft/10m), pegs, two sticks 3ft (1m) long, 12ft (4m) of paracord
KNOTS Siberian hitch (see page 52), double half hitch (see page 52), Prusik (see page 56), clove hitch (see page 51), slippery guy (see page 57)

Step 1
Find two trees about 15ft (5m) apart, lay out the rope and tie a Siberian hitch around one of the trees.

Step 2
Feed the rope through the second row of loops on the tarp lengthways (about a third along). Wrap the rope around the other tree and tie a double half hitch with a bight (quick release).

Step 3
Tie a Prusik knot on each side of the tarp attached to the tent line to secure it in place.

Step 4
Peg down the rear two corners of the longest side of the tarp to form the back of the shelter.

Step 5
With a length of rope, tie a double half hitch to the tarp loop on the front corner of each side.

Step 6
With the same piece of rope, now attached to the tarp, leave a short gap and then tie a clove hitch around one of the 3ft (1m) sticks. Repeat on the other side. These sticks will sit on the ground at the front of the shelter. The tension of the pegged-down rope will secure them.

Step 7
With the rope still tied to the stick, bring it to the ground at about a 45° angle. Push a peg into the ground and tie a slippery guy knot around it with the working end of the rope and tighten. Repeat on the opposite front corner.

3

2

6

4

5

1

7

Tarp bender

This shelter makes a great group den, and is very easy to build. I've used it many times for sleepouts. With a fire outside you can be super-cosy inside.

AGE 6+

TIME 25+ minutes

TOOLS Folding saw, mallet

MATERIALS Tarp, six hazel poles, about 1in (2.5cm) in diameter and 8ft (2.4m) long, string/paracord, one thicker hazel pole about an arm's length long and 3in (8cm) in diameter, 6 pegs

KNOTS Canadian jam knot (see page 58) or square lashing (see page 59)

Step 1
Cut six hazel poles 8ft (2.4m) tall and 1in (2.5cm) in diameter. Cut one thicker hazel pole; about an arm's length and 3in (8cm) diameter. This will be used to make post holes.

Step 2
Make two holes in the ground, using the thicker pole, about 6ft (1.8m) apart. Place two of the 8ft (2.4m) hazel poles into one hole. Twist them together and then bend them over to form an archway. Push the opposite ends into the other hole so that the arch stays upright. This arch will form the doorway.

Step 3
Draw a large semicircle starting from one side of the doorway, curving around back to the other. This marks where the back of the bender will be and should have a radius of about 5ft (1.5m). Along this line, make four more holes in the ground, spaced about 2ft (60cm) from one another and place the remaining four hazel poles into them.

Step 4
Allow the natural curve of the poles to bend towards the doorway. Make sure they are secure in the ground, or the shelter will lift up.

Step 5
Bend each pole inwards towards the doorway.

Step 6
Secure them onto the arch with a Canadian jam knot or square lashing.

Step 7
Throw the tarp over the frame and secure it. Peg it down through the loops at the back.

Lean-to shelter

This is great for group sleepouts, is simple to construct and can be used effectively with a fire outside as it is open on one side. However, it can be time-consuming to complete the final leaf layer and can cause great disruption to the mini-beasts' habitats.

AGE 4+
TIME 45+ minutes
TOOLS Garden sack (optional)
MATERIALS Long poles and sticks, leaves, wood, grasses, string/paracord
KNOTS Timber hitch (see page 54), Canadian jam knot (see page 58), square lashing (see page 59)

Tip
When piling the leaves or grasses on your den, start from the ground and work your way up, making sure there are no gaps.

Step 1
The basic structure is in the shape of a football goal. Find two trees that are far enough apart to fit one person lying down between them.

Step 2
Look for a pole long enough to extend past both trees. Secure the pole to the trees using a Canadian jam knot or a timber hitch. This will be your ridge pole. Make sure the wood is not rotten, as this would make the whole structure weak. This pole needs to sit somewhere between belly button and shoulder height. The lower down the pole, the cosier your den will be, but the more difficult to get in and out of.

Step 3
The tallest person to lies down perpendicular to the ridge pole and with their head under it. Mark out a line where their feet reach. This will indicate how big you need to make the den. Lay sticks up against your ridge pole as close together as you can reaching out to this line. Fill in the sides with sticks too.

Step 4
Once you have finished laying all the poles in place, cover the area in twigs. This will help to stop the leaves falling through.

Step 5
Now insulate and waterproof the shelter by adding a thick layer of dried leaves, twiggy branches, grasses or whatever the woodland floor may offer. Ideally, this layer will reach a depth of fingertip to elbow to be properly effective as a survival den. But if you're only spending one night in it, or just enjoying a day's play, simply cover it in dead leaves or grasses – just enough to fill in the gaps. If you have a garden sack, fill it with leaves and pour them over your den.

Tip
If you're going to spend a night out in your new home, why not try a long log fire (see page 80) to help keep you warm? Remember, if you build yourself a bed with a good pile of leaves or ferns to sleep on, you'll keep much warmer, as you will stop your precious body heat from escaping into the cold ground.

The cave

SHELTERS ARE AN IMPORTANT PART OF OUR LIVES. WE RELY ON THEM EVERY DAY, FROM OUR HOUSES TO UMBRELLAS. BUT I THINK MOST OF US TAKE THEM FOR GRANTED, ASSUMING THAT A SHELTER WILL BE THERE FOR US WHEN WE NEED ONE. I NEVER KNEW JUST HOW IMPORTANT A SHELTER WAS UNTIL I DIDN'T HAVE ONE, IN A STORM, ON A MOUNTAIN, IN THE WILDERNESS.

After days of walking through forest after forest, covered by shadowy trees with little sight of the sky, we suddenly found ourselves with a new view. Our path had taken us to a beautiful sea of meadows, folding into one another, nestled in a dip in between towering grand mountains. We named the place Hidden Meadows and decided to make this our home for a few days while we mended shoes, sanded fish hooks and counted our rations.

"We knew that we could not make it to lower, more protected, ground before the storm hit."

We'd been there for two days and had been anxiously watching a storm encroaching. There was no need to log in or switch on for a weather update here – the surroundings gave us their own minute-by-minute, up-to-date forecast. The mountains turned blacker, the clouds began to look menacing, and the temperature cooled. We knew that we could not make it to lower, more protected, ground before the storm hit.

We longed for our sheltering trees in the forest now. We had no choice but to stay put and find shelter fast.

No trees meant no sticks to build with, but after a few hours of searching we discovered our solution. A boulder the size of a bus had nestled itself firmly in the side of the mountain, creating a deep lip and a cave-like enclosure. It was not a particularly deep cave, but it was a shelter nonetheless.

Taking out the smaller stones from the floor of our new home and repositioning these to make side walls was a relentless task. It took all day and all of our energy, but with the wind gathering power and speed we were spurred on. Hours later, we stood back to admire our survival shelter.

A gust of wind and the ever-darkening sky urged us not to wait to bed down. We stole a coal from our existing fire and carefully carried it across the rocks to our new home to awaken the light in our dark cave. Then we lay like sardines in a very small tin.

My legs were too long to lay straight unless I forced them, this way and that, until they found a nook where they could rest. My arms had to stay by my sides like a soldier on watch and to change positions was a real challenge, moving stones and other people's body parts to fit mine in around them. I did have a 'pillow', which I was smug about, until my ears went numb. I found out that rock pillows have their downfalls! All this discomfort had to be better than being outside in the elements, the freezing rain and gusting wind on top of a mountain.

The fire provided more of a sense of comfort and light then actual heat. A felted woollen blanket was hung in place of a door but acted more like a bellowing sail, giving us an up-to-date forecast of the high winds. We were grateful of our shelter nonetheless. We shared stories, laughed at our situation and fell into a gentle slumber.

A little while later I woke to find the cave dark and quiet. The fire was out and the storm was at its peak. The wind was desperately trying to find a way in and one of my fellow tribesmen was frantically trying to find a way out, yelling and panicking. His anxiety acted like an alarm. I started imagining that the cave was falling in. It was dark, cold and the storm was raging outside, but I needed to get out! We all did!

"It was dark, cold and the storm was raging outside, but I needed to get out!"

We somehow found the way back to our mountaintop camp, battling through the winds, knowing that this was risky but feeling that if we could reawaken our old fire we would feel safe again. We managed to gather enough materials and in no time had a roaring fire. We allowed the wind to weave around us and the thunder to vibrate above us.

I remember the moment the storm cleared. We were relieved to see the stars again in a pitch black sky, no longer gray with anger. We watched in disbelief as rain turned into soft flakes of snow. I pulled my blanket closer to me and thought how grateful I was to have experienced such an intense night. I felt like an animal. A wild creature on top of the mountains, ill-equipped without its fur.

Fire

Fire is an essential part of bushcraft if you are intending to camp out for any length of time. It will provide warmth and a means to cook. Learning to light a fire is a core outdoor skill that teaches children about perseverance as well as science. It is also very satisfying to achieve success. The best way to ensure a great fire is 'proper prior preparation', which should 'prevent poor performance'. Make sure you have gathered enough materials to light your fire first.

Fire safety

Always follow these important rules when lighting fires.

- Seek permission from the landowner first.

- Select a safe fire site. Look up and around. Check that your fire is not at the base of any tree, far away from any roots or overhanging branches.

- Make sure you have a way to extinguish your fire before you begin, such as a bucket of water or a fire extinguisher.

- You can create an obvious area around your fire by placing large logs in a circle around it to prevent children getting too close. Clearly state that they cannot go inside of this log circle unless invited to do so by an adult.

Three ingredients of fire lighting

Fire is like a triangle with equal sides. Each side represents an essential ingredient in fire lighting. Each ingredient must be kept in proportion with the others. Too much fuel will suffocate your flames and put it out. Too much air will blow out your fire. Too much heat will burn it out, while too little will not burn at all.

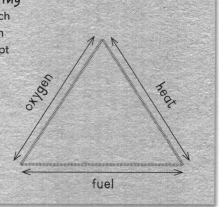

Four methods of fire lighting

There are many different ways to light a fire by harnessing different heat sources, using different methods to create a spark or making enough heat to form an ember. You can use manmade materials or natural resources. Below are four methods to experiment with.

Friction

Friction is the act of rubbing two surfaces together to create heat. There are many friction methods that can be used to light a fire, including a bow drill, hand drill, flint and steel (see page 78), fire plough and fire saw. These methods can be difficult to master and require lots of practice to succeed. Try working together as a team to achieve success. Follow our advice on how to make fire by friction as a group (page 88).

Solar

This method uses the sun's energy and can be harnessed using a reflective device such as a magnifying glass. Place the magnifying glass between the sun and your tinder (King Alfred's cake fungus works well, see page 75). Tilt the magnifying glass to create a small spot of bright light on your tinder. Hold it there until smoke rises. Add your smouldering tinder to a tinder nest and blow into a flame.

Chemical

This is the act of combining materials to create heat or flame. An example of this would be combing potassium permanganate and glycerine (liquid sugar). You can do this safely by adding a little of each to a piece of paper and standing well back.

Electrical

Electrical energy can be used to create a spark. Using wire wool and a live battery is an easy way to light an electrical fire. Using a 9V square battery, rub the wire wool against both elements on one end. The wire wool short-circuits the battery and creates a spark.

Sources of tinder

Tinder is the first material that the flame or spark will contact, therefore it must be absolutely dry and burn immediately. The best way to use many of these natural tinders is to make a tight 'nest' onto which you then drop an ember (see Lighting a fire using a fire steel, page 78).

Seed heads

Cattails (above left) grow in ponds and lakes. Their very fluffy seed heads are great to use for extending your coal and can be used in combination with other tinders to produce a sustainable flame. Clematis (above right) seed heads also make a great tinder, especially as an ember extender.

Bark

This material (left) can burn very hot but may not be easy to get going. Rough it up using the back of a knife or rock to produce fine sawdust, then light it with a spark from the fire steel. Only use bark from dead fallen trees – there is no need to peel bark from a living tree.

Honeysuckle is a woody vine that can be found in lots of woodlands. When harvesting the bark, remove only the outer layers, which offers itself up naturally. The fibres are long and papery, lending themselves to good tinder

bundle construction. Prepare the fibre by making two fists, hold the fibres in both hands and rotate the hands forward. The fibres will break down as they are rubbed together, giving a finer fuel. This material is also the favourite building material of field mice, so only take a little.

Dead bracken

Dead and dried bracken (right) can be used to make a tinder bundle if compacted like a small bird's nest.

Fluff or lint

Fluff or lint (from your pockets or clothes dryer) can be used as tinder and is pretty easy to forage.

King Alfred's cakes

King Alfred's cakes (right), or cramp balls, are rounded black fungi that grow mainly on fallen ash trees. When dried, they act like little coals, taking a spark from your fire steel. They burn slowly, much like a charcoal briquette, with pungent smoke. Fragments can be broken off to expose more embers and be transferred to a tinder bundle to create an open flame.

Char cloth

This is simply cotton or silk scorched black in a tin on a fire (see page 84 to make your own). This is a great tinder and was widely used historically. A spark dropped onto a piece of char cloth will produce an ember, not a flame, until added to a dry tinder nest.

Cotton wool balls

Manmade cotton wool balls are one of my favourite tinders to use. They take a spark quickly and easily, igniting into flames. No nest is required.

Tip
Add a little petroleum jelly to the underside of your cotton wool on a wet day to give your fire a chance to burn longer.

FIREWOOD

All wood burns differently, at different temperatures and speeds. Knowing what wood to choose will help you make an efficient fire. However, as dried or dead wood is best, sometimes nature decides which wood to burn.

Ash

This is one of best woods for burning. It will produce a steady flame and good heat output. It can be burnt when green but, like all woods, burns best when dry.

Beech

This produces a steady flame and a good amount of heat, but burns away quickly.

Hawthorn

This is a good traditional firewood that has a slow burn with good heat output. We have found it to be one of the hottest and therefore great in pizza ovens. We attempted to cook bread in the coals of a hawthorn fire recently, but due to the high level of heat in the coals alone, our bread burnt within minutes.

Larch

Larch produces a reasonable heat output, but needs to be well seasoned. It burns fast and gives good light.

Tip
Best woods for cooking fires:
oak, beech, maple, birch, sycamore.

Best woods for campfires:
ash, fir, apple, hazel, holly.

Use this poem to help you:

These hardwoods burn well and slowly –
Ash, Beech, Hawthorn, Oak, and Holly;

Softwoods flare up quickly and fine,
Birch, Fir, Hazel, Larch and Pine;

Elm and Willow you'll regret,
Chestnut green and sycamore wet.

Scouting Resources
(This poem was written by Celia Congreve and is believed to have been first published in *The Times* newspaper on 2 March 1930.)

Oak

Oak burns long and slow and is very hot. It can be hard to light, but when it gets going it provides an even heat. It is ideal wood for cooking, as it produces little smoke, which makes cooking on a fire pleasurable, and it adds a lovely smoky flavour to some meats and fishes.

Pine

Pine burns with a good flame and produces good heat when seasoned well. It is relatively easy to process, although can be difficult to split due to all the knots. It is especially good to use as a starter wood (for kindling) due to its high content of volatile oils.

Poplar

This is a very smoky wood with a poor burn.

Willow

This is a poor firewood that does not burn well even when seasoned, although it is great as a bow drill wood.

Lighting a fire using a fire steel

A fire steel is a ferrocerium rod that gives off extremely hot sparks (up to 5430°F/3000°C) when it is scraped against a hard, rough surface (usually a piece of steel attached to the rod). Unlike matches or a lighter, fire steels can be used in the wet and claim to have about 12,000 strikes in them.

AGE 5+

TIME 10+ minutes

TOOLS None, but a saw could be handy if you need to cut the wood to size

MATERIALS Fire steel, tinder, dry wood, fire bowl (optional)

Step 1
Find a place to light your fire that follows the safety advice on page 72. Collect dry tinder. This is flammable material that will take a spark easily, such as cotton wool, birch or cherry bark. (See page 74 for a guide on the best tinder to use.)

Step 2
Build a small platform for the fire to sit on. Remember, if you sat straight on the ground after rainfall you'd get a wet and cold bottom, with all of your heat escaping into the ground; it's the same for fire. Just a line of dry sticks will do. You could also use a metal fire bowl, which is useful for not scorching the ground and leaving no trace.

Step 3
Collect large bundles of three different sizes of dry wood:

1) As thin as a matchstick and as long as your arm.
2) As thin as your finger and as long as your arm.
3) As thick as your wrist and as long as your arm.

Tip
If your fire is struggling a little you can gently lift a bundle of sticks from their ends to encourage oxygen to the core of your fire. This should instantly create more flames.

Step 4
A fire steel can be sourced from outdoor shops and online. To use a fire steel, place the striker flat on the top of the ferrocerium rod and use your strength to firmly push them together. Now, still holding that pressure, lift the striker to a 45° angle. Keeping the pressure and angle steady, scrape all the way down with your rod, pinning down the cotton wool to ignite a spark. If you find it difficult to maintain the pressure, start with the striker halfway down the rod. While a fire steel is a great way to start a fire, matches may be appropriate when you don't want to disturb your fire lay. Strike a spark onto your tinder.

Step 5
When the tinder is alight, carefully put on a large bundle of '1s'. Remember – too little and your fire will not take. Lay the 1s carefully on top of your flame. Once you hear a gentle crackle, the fire is starting to take. Lay on another bundle of 1s, holding them carefully at one end. Gently lay these on in a criss-cross fashion, like a waffle or a Jenga stack.

Step 6
Continue layering up the wood like this. Once you have used all the 1s, start adding the 2s in the same way, then gradually your 3s, always considering the fire triangle (see page 72). Lay your 3s to create the fire according to your needs, whether that is warmth or cooking and considering the weather and your situation.

Fire lays

Whether it is for tea making, cooking, for light, a hearth to gather around or to keep myself and a group warm, I never spend a day out in the woods without lighting a fire. How I build that fire depends on what I need to use it for. Below is a guide that will help you decide.

Tipi fire

Use
This is not effective for cooking, as it doesn't create a substantial bed of coals and is not flat, but is effective in creating heat for a group to sit around.

How to
Place a stick upright in the ground. Pack your tinder loosely around this stick. Lay some kindling against the stick at an angle to form a tipi. Keep one side slightly open so that you can light your tinder. Keep leaning up sticks around the core. Light the tinder. The tipi will enable the fire to burn upwards, allowing good draught. Add in the other fuel as the fire gets established.

Criss-cross/ upside-down fire

Use
Good for producing coals for cooking.

How to
This fire breaks the rule of using thin-to-thick materials that start from the bottom; this fire is constructed with the bigger logs at the bottom with kindling and tinder placed above. When the tinder is lit, gravity takes hold and the fire and embers fall onto the fuel below, igniting each consecutive layer as it grows.

Long log fire

Use
This fire is especially good for using in conjunction with natural shelters. If built efficiently and used with a fire reflector, you can keep warm even without a sleeping bag in cold conditions.

How to
The long log fire is made by making three or so small fires in a line. When your fires are burning well, you can start to extend the length by adding additional longer logs and placing them horizontally. The long fire will serve you well in cold temperatures when you need continuous warmth throughout the night. Therefore, you ideally need logs as long as your body to provide maximum warmth. These will burn long and slow and require minimal work once established.

Star fire

Use

This is a great fire if you are leaving base camp for some time and want your fire to continue to hold heat and smoulder until you return. The logs are fed in lengthways and then drawn apart to leave glowing embers and ash (for cooking) in the centre. This type of fire is very useful for conserving fuel. It produces little flame or smoke when required and can be easily stoked by pushing one of the logs inwards occasionally.

How to

A star fire is formed by making a small fire (follow the beginner's guide above) and arranging logs around the outside facing inwards to form the points of a star. To start the fire going strong again, simply push the logs together and blow to add a little oxygen. The long sticks should work as insulation to keep your coals ignited.

V-shaped fire

Use

This fire provides good coals for cooking and can easily sustain itself given the right amount of wood. This method works especially well in windy conditions. Often the wind can cause problems when fire lighting, but this method uses the wind to provoke the fire.

How to

Collect large bundles of kindling as long as your arm from fingertip to elbow at least. Separate your kindling into four good handfuls. Each handful should look like the end of a miniature witch's broom. Think about which way the wind is blowing. Even if there is only a slight breeze, take note. Kneel with your back to the wind and place your handfuls of kindling in a V-shape with the open side of the V facing you, overlapping one another at the tip.

Place your chosen tinder just under the tip of your triangle and light your tinder. I recommend using a match so as not to disturb your sticks.

Keeping the kindling long allows you to adjust the fire as it becomes established. If your fire needs more oxygen, lift the uppermost bundle a little to allow more air into the fire. Layer up dry finger-thick sticks as the fire becomes established.

Tip

A matchstick breaks easily, so when you strike it, apply pressure along its length, not across it. As you strike the match, support the head. Don't be afraid of burning your finger, just remove it at the end of the strike. On igniting the match, take it straight into cupped hands to protect the flame. Once the match is burning, carefully take the flame to the tinder. Do not drop the matchbox and try to avoid it getting wet.

Making charcoal

Charcoal has been used since earliest times for many purposes, including as an art material, as fuel and as medicine. It can be used to filter water, to treat sickness, as a pigment, for heating our houses and for cooking delicious barbecue foods, to name just a few of its uses.

AGE 7+

TIME 30 minutes

TOOLS Secateurs, tool to punch a small hole in the tin lid (nail or screwdriver), small plug to fit inside the hole (a stick will work), tongs or heatproof gloves

MATERIALS Small sticks of hazel or willow about pencil thickness, large biscuit tin (for a smaller batch you could use a golden syrup tin, or similar).

Step 1
Light a fire (see page 78). You want a nice bed of coals to work with so the criss-cross/ upside-down fire (see page 80) would work best. Cut up your sticks. The length will depend on the depth and width of your tin. Cut them to fit inside your tin with the lid on.

Step 2
Punch a hole in the top of your tin to allow the air to escape.

Step 3
Place your sticks inside your tin and nestle it into the coals. The smoke should come out from the hole in a steady stream.

Step 4
Once the smoke stops billowing out, your charcoal should be ready. Using your tongs or heatproof gloves, take the tin off the fire. Immediately plug up the hole – otherwise you risk the material inside combusting when it comes into contact with the oxygen in the air.

Step 5
Leave to cool for 15–20 minutes. See if you can draw a picture with your charcoal. You can practise drawing on rocks for a really authentic-looking picture.

What is charcoal?
There is archaeological evidence of charcoal production going back about 30,000 years. Charcoal is mostly pure carbon, called char, made by cooking wood in a low-oxygen environment, and burning off volatile compounds such as water, methane, hydrogen and tar.

Making char cloth

Char cloth makes an excellent tinder. It is very easy to make using 100% cotton material that has been starved of oxygen and had all of its moisture removed through charring. Char cloth ignites with even the smallest spark and holds a very hot ember. It is commonly used with a flint and steel or ferrocerium rod.

AGE 7+
TIME 30 minutes
TOOLS Scissors, tool to punch a small hole in the tin lid (nail or screwdriver), small plug to fit inside the hole (a stick will work), tongs or heatproof gloves
MATERIALS 100% cotton cloth (such as a tea towel, T-shirt, handkerchief or bandana), large biscuit tin (for a smaller batch you could use a golden syrup tin, or similar).

Char cloth is made using the same principles as charcoal (see page 82), putting the cloth into an almost airtight tin with a small hole in it, and cooking it in campfire coals until the smoking slows and the cloth is completely charred.

Step 1
Light a fire. You want a nice bed of coals to work with so the criss-cross/upside-down fire (see page 80) would work the best.

Step 2
Cut your material into small squares about 1½ x 1½in (4 x 4cm).

Step 3
Place the material inside your tin and nestle it into the coals. The smoke should come out from the hole in a steady stream.

Step 4
Once the smoke stops billowing out, your char cloth should be ready. Using your tongs or heatproof gloves, take the tin off the fire. Immediately plug up the hole, otherwise you risk the material inside combusting when it comes into contact with the oxygen in the air.

Step 5
Leave to cool for 15–20 minutes. Drop a spark onto your cloth and then add to a nice dry tinder bundle to give your fire a great start.

1

2

3

4

5

Tip

Carry your char cloth in a ziplock sandwich bag or small metal tin to prevent it from getting wet.

Carrying fire

Most of us do not consider ourselves reliant on fire but our Stone Age ancestors had a different bond with it. They relied on it for survival, for warmth, for protection, for light and for making food more digestible and water safer to drink.

On our wilderness trip, I re-discovered my bond with fire, depending on it again as our ancestors would have done once.

Every night we used the ancient 'bow drill' method (see page 88), trusting in friction to create a spark. Once the fire was going, we had the means of preparing our meal. We then purified and boiled water to make pine needle tea to soothe us from the inside.

With fire came warmth and the feeling that life was restored. The light from the fire meant the day could be extended, allowing us to continue fixing our shoes, sanding our fish hooks and sharing stories until we could hear our rock pillow calling.

But there were one or two days when rain threatened. Due to forest fires we couldn't always rely on there being wood available so sometimes we chose to carry fire with us (see page 90). We adopted the ancient skill of making a tinder bundle to carry an ember. Our ancestors may have simply used a large smouldering fungus such as King Alfred's cake or dried birch polypore carried with raw hide cordage.

Tip
King Alfred's Cake (see page 75) is a black fungus that grows mainly on fallen ash trees. Inside, it looks exactly like coal and acts the same way too. Trapping heat within its layers, it can smoulder for hours depending on its size. It also acts as a great mosquito repellent if left burning at your base camp.

AGE 9+
TOOLS Tongs or shovel
MATERIALS Bark, dried grasses and leaves, dried fungus (such as King Alfred's cake), An ember, damp cordage or string

Step 1
Collect a combination of some semi-dry grass and leaves and a piece of flexible bark; birch, cedar, etc.

Step 2
Using tongs or a shovel, place the hot coals from your fire directly in the middle of the bark and carefully roll it up tightly around the grass and leaves as if you're making ember sushi. (You can use a King Alfred's cake instead of an ember.)

Step 3
Wrap and tie it as tightly together as possible with some type of cordage, vine, thin green withy or even moistened string or jute.

Step 4
Wait until the bundle begins to smoke and smoulder then pack the ends with moss and dried leaves etc. The bundle must be tight so that it does not get too much oxygen. Too much oxygen will cause it to burn too fast. Occasionally check it to make sure that it is still smouldering. If you need to, waft it in the breeze, swinging it back and forth to allow oxygen back to the coal. Depending on the size of your original coal your bundle could stay smouldering for 5-8 hours if nurtured correctly.

Step 5
Untie the bundle and blow into it to get the flames of your new fire going.

Group bow drill

This is best set up by an adult, but it makes a great group activity with children. Rubbing sticks together to create fire is magic and always gets people excited.

AGE 7+
TIME 1 hour+
TOOLS Saw, knife
MATERIALS
Firewood (dead wood from willow, sycamore, lime, cedar or poplar), green wood for the bearing block/ palm stone, tinder, approx. 30ft (10m) length of rope

Step 1
Saw a piece of dead wood (see materials list) into a plank 1in thick, 12in long and 5in wide (2.5 x 30 x 12.5cm). This will be the hearth.

Step 2
Also using the dead wood, carve a spindle about 15in (38cm) long and about 1in (2.5cm) in diameter and straight. Carve a point at one end and then round off the other end to make a dome shape.

Step 3
Make the bearing block/palm stone from green wood, about 1ft (30cm) long. Carve out a dip in the middle with a knife.

Step 4
At one end of the hearth and about 1in (2.5cm) in from the edge, carve out a dip for the rounded end of the spindle to fit in. The spindle will be rotated back and forth in it.

Step 5
Cut out a V-shaped notch in the hearth to the edge next to the dip you carved. This can be done either with your knife or a saw.

Step 6
Split the group up so that some are kneeling either side of the hearth. Place the rounded end of the spindle into the dip in the hearth and push down onto the pointed end with the bearing block, nestling it into the carved dip. Wrap the rope around the middle of the spindle and have the group pull back and forth until the notch is filled up with charred wood dust. Once the notch is filled, speed up the pulling for 10 seconds. If a continuous rising of smoke is seen from the notch, let the ember sit there for about 10–30 seconds to let it grow.

Step 7
Carefully tip the ember into a tinder bundle and then gently blow on it to make flames.

Carrying the flame

FIRE IS WONDERFUL: IT KEEPS US WARM, SAFE AND NOURISHED. ON OUR WILDERNESS TRIP, I RELIED GREATLY ON FIRE. IT OFFERED ME MANY OF MY BARE NECESSITIES: SAFE WATER TO DRINK; HEAT TO SLEEP COMFORTABLY; THE MEANS TO MAKE A HOT MEAL. IT ALSO GAVE LIGHT SO WE COULD LOCATE THE BEST PATCH OF GROUND TO LAY DOWN A SHEEPSKIN, FIND A SUITABLE ROCK FOR A PILLOW, AND ANOTHER ROCK TO HEAT IN THE FIRE TO USE AS A HOT-WATER BOTTLE.

Of course, there were days when rain threatened. Even though we were surrounded by wood most of the time, there were some days when we couldn't rely on there being fuel available due to forest fires. One particular day stands out.

We were preparing for our departure and carrying out our usual camp-clearing duties to leave no trace of our existence. I went to douse our fire with water taken from the nearby stream when my teacher asked me to wait. She was so accustomed to living out in the wild that she was continuously reading the environment.

"The clouds grew darker and the smell in the air changed to one of wet, freshly turned soil that always comes before a rainstorm."

She had been watching the clouds and sensed that it would rain. To us, the sky looked blue with wispy clouds, but we trusted her instincts. As we couldn't rely on being able to start a fire from our scorched surroundings, she said we should carry fire with us. She showed us how to make a tinder bundle from bark, grasses and moss to carry an ember from our existing fire to our next rest stop.

We packed up and walked through the forest, occasionally wafting our smoking bark cigar through the air to make sure our ember stayed alive. Once again, our terrain changed. There was no more forest, just barren landscape with miles in between trees. We saw a momma bear and cub running in the opposite direction just a few metres ahead of us – it was a gift to see them so clearly with no trees to hide behind. But then the atmosphere changed. A cool wind began to pick up. The clouds grew darker and the smell in the air changed to one of wet, freshly turned soil that always comes before a rainstorm. Sure enough, the heavens opened and rain gushed down.

We were all wearing buckskins from head to toe, which are not the best attire for a rainstorm. They get wet, monstrously heavy and take a long time to dry. I remember thinking how this

"We gathered twigs and sticks from any dry nooks and crannies we could find and soon we had a roaring fire that fought the rain and won."

wasn't like being out for a hike at home, where I would wear a full-on rain jacket knowing that even if I did get wet, I'd be home by the evening with a hot bath, a cup of tea and a blanket, snuggled up on the sofa. This was different. If we got wet, we stayed wet and cold and miserable.

Normally, we would use the overhanging branch of a larch tree as an umbrella when rain threatened, but here there was nothing for miles. I had only rawhide flip-flops between my feet and the slippery ground, and they were rapidly turning into flip-flaps as they reverted back into pieces of soggy flesh. I found myself yearning for a pair of wellies.

We trekked onwards and, as usual, upwards, praying for a tree, a bush, or anything that might offer a little shelter and respite. Our teacher ran on ahead so we might make an informed decision of where to stop. She returned with news of a tree. A small, rather lonely, balding spruce tree, but one that we could all just about fit around the base of if we snuggled tightly together.

We accepted our new home with relief, huddling in close, more grateful than ever before of our bark bundle, which had hugged our precious little ember for miles. We added dry tinder from our fishskin pouches and gave some gentle encouraging breaths to awaken the flames. We gathered twigs and sticks from any dry nooks and crannies we could find and soon we had a roaring fire that fought the rain and won. We made salmon jerky broth and pine needle tea and felt restored. We could feel a few raindrops through the trees' needles, but we were grateful that it could have been a lot worse.

It wasn't until we were about to snuggle down for the night that someone found they were lying right next to a great big bear poop. We looked around us. In our haste to settle in, we had failed to notice that we were surrounded by giant bear poops. Not only had we found the only standing tree in the area, we had found the local bear toilet as well! We looked at one another, looked at our roaring fire and into the rain and laughed, knowing that at least until morning our fire would protect us – although, I have to say, I slept with one eye open that night!

Collecting water

It's easy to find water in streams, rivers, lakes and puddles. But can we drink it? Many people will say 'no, it's dirty!' Or 'no, it's got germs in!' That's true of untreated water, but you could collect water from any of these sources and drink it if it is filtered and purified correctly. So how do we find, collect and make water safe to drink? This section teaches you some handy tricks.

Rainwater collection

There are many simple ways to collect rainwater – in a bucket, cup, mess tin or any other receptacle that can hold a liquid. It's fun to see how many ways you can find to collect water!

Find four stakes about 3ft (1m) long to place in the ground and tie each corner of your tarp to the stakes.

Wait for the rain! Rainwater is only as clean as the vessel that you collect it in, so make sure the tarp is clean as well as the container you use to scoop the water out.

Collecting dew

If you're out camping and wake up early the ground can sometimes be wet with dew. This is fresh water ready to be collected.

Find some long grass. Tie a tea towel or sponges around each of your legs below the knee and walk slowly through the grass.

Squeeze out the collected water. You can turn this into a game and see who can collect the most water. Again, remember that the water you collect is only as clean as the vessel you collect it in.

Birch tapping

Another way to find drinkable liquid is to tap sap from a tree. Sap is delicious, with a slightly sweet taste, and can be drunk straight away. Birch trees (Betula species) *are the best option, but other possibilities are sycamore* (Acer pseudoplatanus), *lime linden* (Tilia), *and maples* (Acer).

AGE 4+
TIME 6–24 hours
TOOLS Secateurs
MATERIALS Plastic bottles, string

Step 1

Find a birch tree that is about 15in (35cm) in diameter with branches that can be reached when standing. With your secateurs, snip the end off a small branch and see if it starts to drip with sap. (This branch will heal over by itself in time.)

Step 2

Tie your bottle to the branch and weigh it down so the bottle is as horizontal as possible. Come back in a few hours to see how much sap has been collected. It is best to leave it overnight if possible.

1

Making birch syrup

You can turn this sap into a syrup: 17 pints (10 litres) of sap makes about 1¾ pints (1 litre) of syrup. To do this, simply boil it down until it thickens. You can even boil it down further to turn it into sugar.

2

Bottle filter

This filter works well with many layers, taking out the big particles of dirt. It won't remove chemicals or bacteria, however: you will need to kill the bacteria by boiling the water. The combination of filtering and boiling the water makes it safe to drink.

AGE 6+
TIME 20 minutes
TOOLS Scissors
MATERIALS Plastic bottles, piece of cloth, crushed charcoal, gravel, grass, leaves, wood shavings, pine cones (you do not need all the materials listed here, just a combination of small and some large materials so that different layers can be added)

Step 1
Gather all the materials you will need.

Step 2
Cut the bottom off the plastic bottle and remove the lid. Wedge the cloth into the neck of the bottle, then fill it with layers in this order: charcoal, gravel, grass and leaves, wood shavings, pine cones. Make sure everything is compacted down tightly. It is important to keep the layers in this order: the large particles in the water will be filtered out first through the pine cones, while the final layers of crushed charcoal will remove the smaller bits of debris and clean the water.

Step 3
Pour your muddy water slowly through the filter. Be careful not to spill it over the edges, as this will contaminate your clean water. Pass it through the filter several times. If you want to use this water for drinking you will need to heat it to a rolling boil to kill any potentially harmful germs.

Camp craft

Camp craft refers to any skills or practice that you may need whilst camping and is to improve and enhance your time spent outdoors. It is all about 'knowing' how to live comfortably and confidently outside. Your camp should be a place where you feel comfortable, even when far off the beaten track. It is a place where you can rest, plan and prepare for future activities.

Cordage

Making cordage from natural materials is very simple. There are many materials you can use to create strong cordage, which is used for securing shelters, bow strings, bow drill fire making, fishing line, tying up a tarpaulin and weaving pots, to name a few. In this example, we are using stinging nettles (Urtica dioica).

AGE 6+
TIME 15 minutes (plus overnight drying)
TOOLS Protective gloves, rock, piece of wood
MATERIALS Nettles

Step 1
Harvest the nettles in late summer or early autumn, when they are fully mature or over 3ft (1m) tall. Find a good patch of nettles that are tall and straight. With a gloved hand, start from the root and pull the nettle through your gloved hand to strip off the leaves. Repeat this two or three times to remove all of the leaves and the fine, hair-like stings.

Step 2
Cut off the root and tip. Place on a piece of wood and gently break the stalk with a rock.

Step 3
Open the nettle flat to show its inner bark.

Step 4
Bend the stem in half to break the inner bark. Place the outer fibres between your middle finger and index finger and separate the fibres. Do this for about ten nettle strands.

Step 5
Hang the fibres up to dry. When you use them, rehydrate them for 20–30 minutes. Use as many fibres as you wish. Use strands that are equal in thickness for a nice neat string.

Step 6
Find the middle of the length of the fibres. Slightly off the centre point, pinch with both hands then twist in opposite directions to form a loop. While holding the loop, twist the top fibres forwards and bring the bottom fibres over the top. Keep going until you have your required length of cordage.

Strong and medium-strength fibres
Here are suggestions for plants that make strong or medium-strength cordage. When harvesting, take only what you need, and pick from many different plants rather than from just one area.

Strong fibres	**Medium-strength fibres**
Stinging nettle	Inner willow bark
Lime bark (rotted in water and inner fibres peeled)	Honeysuckle bark (shedding bark fibres)
Rosebay willowherb (outer fibres; prepare in a similar way to nettles, gather in winter)	Clematis bark
	Inner elm bark
Sinews	Inner sweet chestnut bark
Horsehair	

1

2

Tip
To add extra fibres (splicing), pick three more strands that are equal in size and thickness to the strands already used. Bend them off centre and add them into your existing string with the bend in the V of the fibres. Keep twisting the fibres till you have your desired length.

3

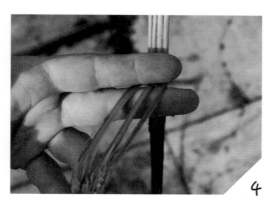

4

5

6

Treating the cordage
When you use material in its living form, initially it will have enough food to live for a while, but this will eventually run out and the material will start to break down. Once you have made your cordage, you can add tallow or beeswax to keep it usable, soft and supple. This is somewhat like leather shoes that we need to wax and polish to 'feed' the leather and stop it deteriorating.

Giant grass rope

This is one of our favourite activities to do with groups. It shows them that one strand of grass may not be very strong but that many strands brought together can be strong enough to use as a rope swing or even to pull a car!

AGE 4+
TIME 20 minutes
MATERIALS Grass

Tip
If the grass has any weak spots, add in more over the weak spot and twist.

Step 1
Collect grass that is no shorter than your fingertips to elbow; the longer, the better.

Step 2
Lay out two lines of grass opposite each other. When laying the grass, overlap the strands.

Step 3
Divide the group in two and have each side kneel down facing each other on the outside of the grass.

Step 4
Have the team on your left carefully twist the grass clockwise (away from them) and the group on the right twist the grass clockwise (towards themselves). This helps bind the fibres.

Step 5
Once all the grass has been twisted, you can pick up the ends and hold them together firmly. Keep the teams twisting the grass clockwise. As they twist the grass, you turn the ends clockwise. The grass will now be turning into rope. Keep doing this until you get to the end.

Variations
Use the rope for a tug of war, to make a rope swing or even a skipping rope.

1

2

3

4

5

Knife safety

Knives are a very important tool in the outdoors, and allowing your child to have one is a big step. When the time comes, explain to your child the seriousness and responsibilities that come with having a knife. Mastering knife skills takes time, so practise as often as you can with simple projects.

Knife use safety brief

For every session when we use knives we give this simple safety brief:

- Show everyone the first-aid kit and where it is kept and have a cuts box with plasters in.

- Make sure everyone knows what the safety bubble is: when sitting, carvers should have no one within an outstretched arm's distance of them, including behind them.

- Always cut away from your body and gripping hand.

- Never move around from your carving spot with an unsheathed knife. Put the sheath on.

- If you cut yourself, STOP and let someone know, no matter how small the cut.

- Your knife is your responsibility.

- Focus on what you are doing and take your time.

- For novice carvers, rest if your hands get tired.

- Always put the knife in its sheath; never dig it into the ground or a log.

Whenever we run a carving course, whether for adults or children, we carry plasters because cuts do happen – I still cut myself sometimes while carving. However, with safe knife techniques we want to minimize the risk of serious cuts.

Always have a good working area on stable ground, try to avoid working with a knife if it is really wet, and always carry a first-aid kit with plenty of plasters.

It is a good idea for children to understand how to use their first-aid kits and what to do if they cut themselves. Teach them this: apply pressure – elevate – pack wound.

Tip
A sharp knife is always safer than a blunt knife. Look after your tools and they will look after you.

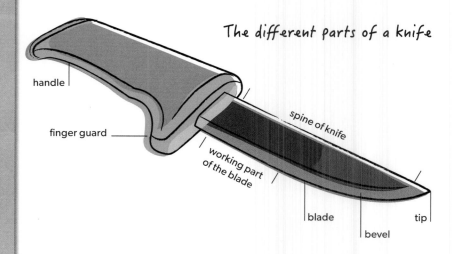

The different parts of a knife

handle

spine of knife

finger guard

working part of the blade

blade

tip

bevel

Safe ways to grip a knife

When carving, we work with the part of the blade closest to the handle. We usually mark the knife blade with a whiteboard pen, about 1in (2.5cm) away from the handle. This gives a visual indicator of the working part.

Fist grip
The fist grip is a secure way to hold your knife that will give you confidence in each cut or carving. This the best way to hold your knife.

Push cut
A push cut can be used for small cuts in a very controlled manner.

Knee brace
The knee brace is a very safe and controlled way to use a knife but it takes getting used to.

Splitting a stick

There are many reasons why you may need to split a stick: to place in an arrow tip, to cook fish or meat on a fire, or to use for weaving, for example. Splitting a stick with a knife in the correct form is very safe. We use two methods.

Method 1
Start with a fist grip but use your thumb and forefinger to grip the wood and apply downward pressure while rocking the knife back and forth. The knife will only go as deep as the blade.

Method 2
Start by placing the blade on the stick and then baton your knife down. Once the split is about 6in (15cm) long, take out the knife and resheath it. Then split the rest by hand. If the split wanders off centre, bend the thicker side to bring it back.

Sharpening a knife

There's a saying that you are only as sharp as your knife. A blunt knife is a hazard, so keeping your knife sharp and well looked after is essential.

Step 1

For knife sharpening we mainly focus on the bevel. This is the part of the blade that angles down towards the cutting edge. You need to remove metal from both sides of the bevel in order to form a fine edge where they meet.

Step 2

Find a flat surface to work on. If you are outdoors, a chopping block is ideal.

Step 3

Start with the knife placed on the end of the stone nearest to you. With the cutting edge facing away from you, tilt the knife until you achieve the correct bevel angle. Place your knife flat on your sharpening stone, then tilt the knife towards the cutting edge until the bevel is lying flat on the stone.

Step 4

Move the knife away from you up the stone, applying gentle pressure with your fingers. Do this twice from the bottom to the top of the stone. Turn the knife over and repeat. At this point, focus on sharpening the blade from the handle through to the first two-thirds of the blade. Sharpen the tip separately. Repeat this process on both sides approximately 10–20 times each side depending on how blunt your knife is.

Step 5

Now sharpen the tip. Put the tip of the blade on the sharpening stone with the bevel lying flush on the stone and push through to the end tip. Repeat on each side approximately 10–20 times. As you take metal off each bevel,

AGE 7+
TIME 5–10 minutes
TOOLS Diamond sharpening stone, flat surface (table or chopping board), old leather belt
MATERIALS Piece of paper

you create a very thin foil of metal where the bevels meet. This is formed by pushing the metal one way then the other as you alternate sharpening strokes. This is referred to as a burr. If you run your thumb down the bevel (towards the sharp edge, not away from it) you can feel this catch a little on the ridges in your thumbprint. To check for this burr visually, turn towards the light and angle the knife, checking for reflections from flat spots that indicate any blunt areas. A sharp edge will reflect very little light.

Step 6

To smooth the edge and remove any remaining burrs, strop your knife. To do this, simply use a leather belt. Sit on a tree stump or chair, attach the belt around your foot and hold the tail end in your other hand. Brush the knife backwards and forwards to remove any burr from the blade. Alternate the stropping strokes back and forth. Around 50 strokes is usually enough.

Step 7

Your knife should now feel razor-sharp. A final test of sharpness is to slice the edge off a sheet of paper.

Tip

Where metal has been removed from the bevel it will show as scratches or shiny areas. If your technique is correct, you will see metal has been removed from the whole bevel. If not, adjust the angles as necessary. You can draw on your knife with a permanent black pen, colouring in the bevel so that you can clearly see if your technique is even. The pen mark should be removed evenly from the entire bevel.

Carving a butter knife

This is a great activity to practise your carving techniques and strengthen your carving muscles. Carving is a great way to focus the mind while learning a new set of skills. Even the wildest group of kids can become quiet and focused when given the task of whittling a butter knife.

Knife safety
Follow the knife safety rules on page 100 before you start.
Children should ALWAYS be supervised by an adult.

AGE 7+

TIME 1 hour minimum

TOOLS Fixed-blade knife

MATERIALS Piece of green hazel (*Corylus avellana*) or sycamore (*Acer pseudoplatanus*), thumb-width and as long as your wrist to the top of your middle finger

KNIFE TECHNIQUES Fist grip, push cut and knee brace (see page 101)

Step 1
Using the fist grip, start carving the stick, taking off small slithers of wood on one side. You can use the knee brace cut to help remove larger pieces.

Step 2
Turn over the stick and carve the other side, taking off small slithers and being careful not to cut too close to the pith (centre of the stick). Always carve away from your gripping hand.

Step 3
Carve a rounded curve using the push cut at the tip of the butter knife.

Step 4
Turn the butter knife around and carve the handle, rounding the ends with a push cut.

Tip
Leave the wooden blade to dry for about a week in a cool place, then sand.

Leather tinder pouch

Once upon a time, our cavemen ancestors would probably have carried a tinder pouch much like we carry our phones and bags – as an item of great importance in our daily lives. Without tinder they would not have had dry materials to start their fire, cook a meal, make water safe to drink, keep warm and so on. Even though it might not be a matter of survival today, it is a good idea to collect tinder when you see it. I always have a pouch full of cattail seed heads, dried clematis, honeysuckle bark, dried mosses and grasses ready for when I might need them.

AGE 8+
TIME 2 hours+
TOOLS Pencil, scissors, stitching needles (glovers' needles for leather), leather hole punch, hammer
MATERIALS
Cardboard, waxed stitching thread, thong for drawstring (either cut the edge of your leather about 1/8in (3mm) thick in a long line or buy pre-bought thong), leather (chamois or leather offcuts will work), PVA or wood glue

Step 1
Make a template from thin cardboard by drawing around a plate about 10in (25cm) in diameter. Draw round the template onto the back of your leather piece, then cut out the circle.

Step 2
Now cut out your second piece. This needs to be 12in (30cm) long from tip to tip and 2in (5cm) wide. The circle in the middle should be 3in (7.5cm) in diameter, although this does not need to be exact. Draw around a cup for the circle shape in the middle. You can embellish this second piece with bits of contrasting leather to add a decorative finish; glue them on with PVA or wood glue.

Step 3
Fold your cardboard template in half four times to give you 16 folds. Mark a dot at the end of each line and use this to mark where the holes in the leather should go. Use a hole punch to make 16 holes. If your leather is thin enough you might be able to use a paper hole punch; otherwise, use a leather punch and hammer. Your holes will need to be at least 3/8in (1cm) away from the edge.

Step 4
Add a little glue to your middle piece to secure it in place. This will help you when you are sewing. Cut a 3ft (1m) length of the waxed thread. Tie a knot at one end and sew your leather strip down the centre of your larger circle. You can do this with a simple running stitch.

Step 5
To finish your stitch, work through the last two stitch holes twice.

Step 6
You will need to re-punch the two holes that are now covered by the middle piece.

Step 7
Thread the drawstring through the right-hand hole and leave a 5in (12.5cm) tail. Then thread the rest in and out of the punched holes and pull up to form your pouch. All you need to do now is to gather some tinder to go inside.

Tip
You can use neatsfoot oil to waterproof the pouch. You can customize the pouch by adding beads or a toggle to the ends of your drawstring.

Wilderness survival

Whether at home or out and about in the woods knowing basic first aid techniques will make you feel safer and more confident in any situation and increase the chances of a happy outcome.

Knowing how to use the materials and equipment around you is not only useful but fun to learn, too. This can easily be combined with other team-building challenges.

Making stretchers

Making these stretchers fosters teamwork and communication as well as the challenge of making the stretchers. Give the group a scenario that includes a rescue mission where they have to make a stretcher and carry a casualty.

AGE 6+
TIME 45 mins+
TOOLS None
MATERIALS Tarp, rope, jackets, two strong poles 7ft (2.1m) long, roll mat
KNOTS Clove hitch (see page 51)

Rope stretcher

Step 1
Lay down two strong poles about an arm's length apart on the ground. Tie a clove hitch at one end of the poles. Take the rope over and under each pole so it forms a zigzag.

Step 2
Finish with another clove hitch and lay the roll mat on top of the rope. You can now carry your casualty.

1

2

FOREST SCHOOL ADVENTURE

Tarp stretcher

Step 1
Lay out the tarp. Place a pole across the width of the tarp two-thirds from one end and then fold the other third of tarp back over the pole.

Step 2
Place a second pole up against the edge of the tarp where it has been folded in and then fold the remaining third of tarp back over both poles. You are now ready to carry your casualty.

Jacket stretcher

Step 1
Lay two poles down next to each other. Do the jackets up and pull the arms inside. Insert the poles into the arms, repeating with more jackets until the poles are covered.

Step 2
You can now carry your casualty.

Plants for wilderness first aid

There are many plants around us that we can use to help heal ourselves. Knowing which ones you can use and what to do with them can mean easing a nettle or bee sting quickly, or slowing down a bleeding wound.

Plantain

(Plantago major)

What it is and where to find it
Plantain is a common weed that can most likely be found in your back garden.

Appearance
The leaves are green, egg-shaped and grow in a rosette with thick stems that meet at a base. When the stems are broken, they reveal stringy veins. The flowers grow on a leafless stalk and the seed head looks like a cat's tail.

How to use
With its antibacterial and anti-inflammatory properties, plantain is magical at treating bites and stings. Pick the leaves, chew up in your mouth or crush with a splash of cold water and apply to the affected area. This is called a compress and works immediately on nettle stings.

Tip
Plantain is far superior to dock leaves for treating nettle stings. Get to know this useful plant and you will see it everywhere.

Safety
Remember if you're not absolutely sure what something is, don't pick it.

Common yarrow

(Achillea millefolium)

What it is and where to find it
Yarrow is a common weed that grows freely in grassland and roadsides.

Appearance
Yarrow leaves look like little feathery ferns. Its tiny white flowers form clusters at the top of the plant.

How to use
With its antibacterial, analgesic and anti-haemorrhagic (sealing of blood vessels) properties, yarrow is great at helping to stop minor wounds from bleeding. It also numbs pain and helps speed up the healing process. Simply pick and crush leaves by hand and pack them onto the wound. You can use a bandage to hold the yarrow in place.

Signal fire

This is a great activity that is quick and fun but could be a vital piece of knowledge in a survival situation. Pretend you are lost in the wilderness: the only way to be found is by making a signal fire. Lots of green grasses and leaves will make thick smoke that can be seen for miles around.

AGE 5+
TIME 20 minutes
TOOLS Fire steel
MATERIALS Cotton wool, silver birch bark, grasses or green leaves, small dry sticks and thin twigs made into a big bundle

Step 1
Lay your sticks down on the ground in a criss-cross pattern. Make sure you are in a safe area to light this fire, with nothing hanging from above and at least 6ft (2m) away from any tree.

Step 2
Place the cotton wool on top of the sticks and then the silver birch bark around it. Finish off with the big bundle of twigs.

Step 3
Cover with the green leaves.

Step 4
Light the cotton wool with the fire steel and watch the smoke rise and become very thick.

Precautions
Be aware that a signal fire will create thick smoke that could cause a hazard to other people. Make sure you are not right next to a road and always ask the landowner's permission before making a fire.

Primitive skills

Our ancestors invented all of the tools we have today. Their methods were a lot more basic than ours and they used the materials they had access to. Many of the tools we use today make the job in hand much quicker but sometimes learning and mastering the process is the real skill. It may take a whole day to achieve a finished project but the level of satisfaction in completing the process is great. After all, our hands are the best tools we own... let's learn how to use them!

Slate arrow

Here we show you how to use slate to make an arrow tip that can be secured onto a stick with pine pitch glue. These days, most of us don't need to hunt to survive, but we can still enjoy the art, skill and fun involved in using a bow and arrow, as long as we know how to use them safely.

AGE 7+
TIME 30 minutes minimum
TOOLS Sharp stone for scoring the shape, hard stone for hammering, sandstone or other abrasive rock, knife
MATERIALS Piece of slate (approx. 2 x 2in/5 x 5cm and ¹⁄₈in/3mm thick), hazel stick (approx. 18in/45cm long and ³⁄₈in/1cm diameter), pine pitch glue (see page 114)

Step 1
Find a hammer stone. This is a stone that is harder than your slate piece. A round heavy one is best. Put your slate on something hard with the bits you wish to break off overhanging. Use your hammer stone to tap slate off until you have a rough arrow shape.

Step 2
Depending on where you live, sandstone should be easy to find once you know where to look for it. It can be pinkish in colour and sometimes crumbly and we often find it in woodlands. Any abrasive rock will also work, even an old brick will do the job. Use this stone like sandpaper, sanding down the rough edges until you have an arrow shape.

Step 3
Cut a step into the thinner end of the hazel stick. Cut about one third of the way through the thickness of the stick ³⁄₄in (2cm) from the end. Carve from this cut towards the end using a push cut (see page 101). Re-heat your pine pitch glue and dab it in the step cut. Push the slate arrowhead onto the glue to fix it on.

Step 4
Finish by tying the arrowhead down with string. When you have wrapped your string around the arrow, dab a bit of pine pitch glue on to stop it unravelling.

Safety note
These slate arrows are not designed for hunting with; they are only models. Also note that slate can be brittle and could easily break if thrown at anything.

Tip
Slate sheets are easy to find. Many builders' merchants have broken ones that they sometimes give away for free. Use the thinner sheets, as the thick ones have multiple layers that can be harder to work with.

1

2

3

4

Pine pitch glue

Humans have used resins for thousands of years for many purposes, including waterproofing, varnishing, gluing, incense and medicines. It is only recently that we have started using synthetic resins. Pine pitch glue is surprisingly strong and works as well as any modern glue. The best part is that it's 100% natural and you can make it yourself!

Tip
The cleaner your resin, the stronger the glue will be.

AGE 10+

TIME 30 minutes (not including foraging for the resin)

TOOLS Pestle and mortar or large round rock, stove top or fire, old saucepan, old sieve

MATERIALS 4tbsp (70ml) pine resin, 4tbsp (70ml) beeswax pastilles, 2tbsp (35ml) ground-up fine charcoal (the finer the better), large flat rock for outside cooking or an old saucepan for inside cooking

Step 1
Finely grind the charcoal using a pestle and mortar or a large round rock. The charcoal makes the glue less sticky to touch and less brittle.

Step 2
Using a low flame and an old saucepan, place the resin in the pan to melt slowly. If you are using foraged resin, you will need to pour it through an old sieve to separate any large bits of bark or general debris. When the resin is clear, heat it up slowly again. Be careful: if the mixture overheats it could lose its best qualities.

Tip
As an alternative to charcoal, you could use sawdust, ground eggshells, bone dust, animal hair or even ground-up rabbit poop (don't use the kitchen pestle and mortar for this!).

Using pine pitch glue
Pitch pine glue can be used for many different things, including sticking feathers on arrows or fixing arrow heads on spears. It is so useful it can be used for almost anything that you want to patch or glue in the woods.

Step 3
Slowly add the beeswax pastilles. You want a 50/50 mix of resin and beeswax. This adds elasticity and makes the glue flexible.

Step 4
Take the mixture off the heat. Let it cool slightly, then add the charcoal.

Step 5
Once the mixture is well combined, find a stick and allow the mixture to collect and cool layer by layer around it, in a sort of gluey version of candyfloss. Allow it to cool completely. It should cool to a solid form on your stick. The stick can then be heated when you wish to use the glue, dabbing on a little at a time.

Harvesting pine resin
To make pine pitch glue, you will need to harvest or source some pine resin. Pine trees produce resin to heal themselves when they have been damaged or when a branch has been broken off. It seals over wounds and protects the tree from infections and pests. The resin looks like yellowish sugar crystals and feels tacky. Quite often when you find the resin it will be dry; therefore you should be able to break it off easily, either with your fingers or with a stick.

1

2

3

4

5

Atl atl and spear

An atl atl is a spear thrower that our ancestors used to hunt with. The spear is attached to the atl atl and launched into the air, much like the device that dog owners use to throw balls long distances.

Step 1

Cut two pieces of hazel: one that looks like a number 7 and a spear that is 5ft (1.5m) long.

Step 2

Carve a point on the spear (long stick) using your carving knife. Making sure you are a safe distance from anyone else and in a safe sitting position with your elbows firmly on your knees. Use the fist grip (see page 101) to take off wood all the way around on one end of the stick to make it pointed. Don't jam the knife in; just take off small bits at a time.

AGE 7+
TIME 30 minutes
TOOLS Knife (see page 100 for knife safety)
MATERIALS Hazel: one spear 5ft (1.5m) long and one stick that looks like a number 7, feathers, string, pine pitch glue (see page 114)

Step 3

Make two push cuts (see page 101) opposite each other, leaving a flap of wood for the feathers to fit in. Make these at the opposite end to the point of the spear.

Step 4

Heat your pine pitch glue and attach your feather into the folds of wood.

Step 5

Tie your string around the base of the feathers and over the glue. Use a dab of glue to hold your string in place.

Step 6

For the atl atl itself (the 'number 7' stick), cut it to arm's length and sharpen the point of the smaller branch (the tip of the number 7) using the same safe technique you used to make your spear. This is where the spear attaches. You will need to push this number 7 end slightly into the non-pointed end of your spear so there is a little indent in which it can sit.

Gone fishing

PEOPLE OFTEN ASK US IF WE WERE HUNGRY WHEN WE LIVED IN THE WILDERNESS AND I ALWAYS ANSWER THE SAME WAY: 'HAVE YOU BEEN HUNGRY TODAY?' OF COURSE WE WERE HUNGRY. I GET HUNGRY BETWEEN BREAKFAST AND LUNCH EVEN WHEN NOT EXERTING MYSELF!

In the wilderness it was a different story. We were constantly moving, continually using our precious energy stores to look for food and burning fats foraging for materials for fire – so, yes, we did find ourselves hungry from time to time. And so we ate. We hunted, we foraged and we fished.

"I had images of me catching fish after fish and cooking them all on a primitively sparked fire."

When we first started planning our adventure, one of the things that excited me most was the prospect of preparing and eating a 100% primitive meal, from nature straight to my belly without any modern interjections. I planned to make my own fish hook from bone and fishing line from natural cordage. I had images of me catching fish after fish and cooking them all on a primitively sparked fire. No waste, no leftovers and licking my fingers the only washing up needed.

I spent days crafting my hook from a buffalo rib bone, sanding it down with sandstone, and twisting dog bane and horsehair into cordage for my fishing line. With a pump drill, I made a hole in the hook through which to thread my leader line, and I waited for the day when I could put it to the test.

We had been walking for hours: 50-pound packs on our back, the sun beating down on us, our bare feet carrying us forwards, our bellies rumbling, echoing through the forest. The berries we'd eaten for breakfast had long ago been digested and the need to eat something more substantial was growing. Then, as if my prayers had been answered, we came over the final ridge for the day and were greeted with the most beautiful sight: a glistening turquoise lake, so clear it was almost translucent. In it we could see fish darting around – lots of delicious-looking fish! The only problem was that the fish could see us, too. Catching one would not be easy, but our hungry bellies urged us to rise to the challenge.

With the perfect handcrafted fishing kit in hand, all I needed was bait. This was a whole other challenge. We hid in and

"we could see fish darting around – lots of delicious-looking fish!"

among long grasses, trying to capture grasshoppers to use as lures. Concealing ourselves from people wearing buckskins was one thing; hiding from a grasshopper was another contest entirely. We had transitioned from being ninjas of the forest to looming, clumsy giants in deerskin clothing. Hours later, however, the headless grasshoppers were attached to our hooks, our lines attached to sticks and we were steadying ourselves in a firm position, allowing the hook and bait to drop into the transparent water. Our teacher, Lynx Vilden, showed us her fishing technique, aptly named 'the Vilden Fling'.

The steady position is important, as when a fish does bite, your movement must be fluid and quick. As soon as you sense a bite, you fling the entire line behind you and hope the combination of speed and bemused fish means you have dinner waiting on the rocks behind. Unfortunately, the reality was that we often ended up in the water and the fish ended up with our hard-earned grasshopper in his mouth! But once – just once – I got lucky.

I watched in silent, ravenous anticipation as a fish approached my bait. The bite came. With one smooth movement I yanked my line from the water and flung it behind my head, hoping that the fish had landed obediently behind me.

"With one smooth movement I yanked my line from the water and flung it behind my head, hoping that the fish had landed obediently behind me."

And there it was: my first trout. Not exactly the haul of fishy treats I had dreamed of, but dinner nonetheless!

I ran back to my tribe, proud of my success. Our fire was awakened and fed with dry wood ready for our micro fish feast. The fish was gutted and cooked straight on the coals. The skin, bones, head and all were gratefully consumed. Nothing was wasted. One fish between six and everyone was fighting for the good bits – the tiny fish brain, the slimy eyes, the crispy skin and the crunchy bones. My partner Dan enjoyed his bit of the fish while drying off sopping buckskins by the fire after a rather embarrassing wrestle with a fish. The fish had won that time.

Fat lamps

Thousands of years ago, fat lamps were used to create light in dark caves for our Stone Age ancestors. They continued to be used into the nineteenth century and beyond.

AGE 7+
TIME 10+ minutes
TOOLS Just your hands!
MATERIALS Air-dry clay, a fat source such as coconut oil, lard or sunflower oil, jute string, lighter/match

Step 1
You will need a small ball of clay, about the size of a lemon. With one hand supporting the bottom of the ball, push your thumb in the middle to make an indent. Use your thumb and forefinger to pinch and bring up the sides to make a pot shape. Smooth away any cracks with a dab of water. Too much water will collapse the pot though, so go easy.

Step 2
Thin out the walls, making sure they are reasonably thick at the top of the pot so it is sturdy.

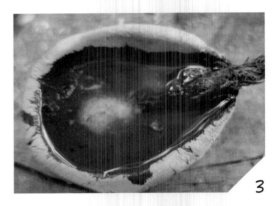

Step 3
Gently pinch a lip into which the wick can sit to be able to draw up the fat. To do this, first slightly moisten the area where you are making the spouted lip. Using two fingers, pull the clay out gently into a small-channelled spout. Support the rest of the pot while doing this so as not to split the bottom.

Step 4
Choose your oil. I like coconut oil: it has many different uses including as a fuel. It will burn well even in solid form. Otherwise, lard and sunflower oil are good, too. You can add the oil in solid form; it does not have to be melted or liquid, as this will happen as it burns. Half-fill your pot with your chosen oil. Lay the wick in the oil, with one end resting on the spouted lip, and light. Use your fingers to lightly dab some oil on the exposed end of the wick. The wick should now draw the oil up and remain lit until the oil burns out.

Tip
You can use a number of different materials for wick: moss, jute, string, various barks (pounded, softened and twisted), cotton wool, or grasses. Rosebay, willow or sedge grass will work, as these have a spongy centre that when pre-soaked in oil stays alight for around 20 minutes.

Nut lamps

Nuts and seeds offer us useful oils for cooking (sesame, walnut, sunflower, etc.), but they can also be used to make little lamps. If you're anything like me, you don't go anywhere without a bag of trail mix, so will always have the materials you need to make one.

AGE 6+

TIME 10 minutes preparation

TOOLS Pounding rock, wooden chopping board or flat rock, lighter or matches

MATERIALS Nuts with a high oil content such as walnuts, pecans, hazelnuts or Brazil nuts

Step 1

Choose your nuts – the fresher the better and in their shells if possible. You only need two or three for each lamp. Find a flat rock or chopping board. You'll need a good, round pounding stone for this next part. With the shells taken off, crush up the nuts into a fine paste. If they are fresh enough you should start to see the oils coming out pretty quickly.

Step 2

Once the nuts have been pounded into a paste, form the paste into a small pyramid shape on the flat rock or chopping board and light the top. It's as simple as that. You will be amazed how long they burn!

1

2

Ancient light

Archaeologists have found limestone and sandstone rocks chipped away to create a small dip in which oil would have been burnt, and these date back at least 40,000 years. Our Stone Age ancestors would not have wasted anything, especially when using animals for survival. They would have used their meat, fur, bones and their fat. This is what they used to burn in their lamps.

Some of these fat lamps were found in caves along with ancient cave art. It is believed that, with the use of torches and fat lamps, the images would appear more alive. With the glow of a flickering light, deer would leap, horses would run and hunters with spears would vibrate with life. Along with an excitable storyteller, these pictures might have been like early movies.

Grass mat

Sometimes, on a cold day when a sit spot calls, or if I'm going camping or spending time outdoors, especially after rainfall, I wish I had something to sit on; something that I didn't have to worry about getting dirty or wet, and something light to carry and easy to pack in a rucksack. A woven grass mat is a perfect solution. It's easy to make, easy to transport and easy to replace when necessary.

AGE 6+
TIME 1 hour
TOOLS Saw, secateurs, scissors, knife
MATERIALS Hazel sticks x 7, 2ft (60cm) long, plenty of long grass, string or paracord

Step 1
To make a mat, you first need to make the loom, using sticks and string or cord. You can use any straight sticks you can find, pushed into the ground to stand alone upwards. I would recommend using at least six sticks at least 2ft (60cm) long, but it depends on the size of your planned project.

Step 2
Each stick has its pair on the opposite side. The distance these are apart from one another is determined by the size you want your project to be. For a simple sit mat I would recommend they are 2ft 6in (76cm) apart. Tie a length of string or paracord between each pair to connect them. This is your weft.

Tip
You can use other grasses and reeds, and even hay or straw if you don't have access to long grass.

Step 3
Tie an additional length of string to each stick on one side, but do not connect to the opposite pair. Instead, connect the loose ends to another stick. This is your weaving bar; it should be a few inches longer than the width of the row of stakes.

Step 4
Lift the weaving bar up above the weft to reveal a gap. Place long bundles of your chosen fibre on top of the weft and lower the weaving bar. This becomes your 'warp'.

Step 5
Repeat by alternately lifting and lowering the weaving bar, adding more warp fibres each time. The closer together the warp, the stronger and thicker your mat will be.

Stone Age weaving
Our Stone Age ancestors would have been keen weavers, using the fibres of plants and the hides and sinews of animals to weave to create the necessities of life. Weaving a grass mat is one way we can recreate their experience.

1

2

Tip
You could also use your loom to weave a survival blanket or mattress, a cloak or a roof for a shelter.

3

4

5

Natural clay

Our ancestors would have relied on clay pots for cooking, for boiling water, for making medicinal broths and more. The clay would have been taken from the ground and moulded into round-bottomed pots, using coils of clay built on top of one another (see page 128). Our ancestors would then have used blazing-hot fires to fire their pottery to make it strong. There are many cultures around the world that still use this process today.

AGE 8+
TIME Between 1 hour and 2 days
TOOLS Bucket to collect the clay in, sieve or muslin cloth, old bedsheet, large stones or a pestle and mortar to grind with
MATERIALS Natural clay, coarse sand, brick or shells

Find a good source of clay in nature. It can often be found near riverbeds; look out for milky-looking water. Clay ranges in colour from reds and oranges to greys and whites. You will know when you find clay due to its distinctive, slippery feel. To test your sample, add water until it has a dough-like consistency, roll it into a long worm about 3/8in (1cm) in diameter and wrap it around your finger. If it begins to break, this indicates that you might want to find some better clay.

What clay to use

All clays, whether found in nature or bought from a shop, are different and so respond differently when handled, moulded, dried and fired.

Two of the most important characteristics to consider when working with clay are shrinkage (the clay can shrink and crack when it dries) and the ability to withstand sudden temperature changes. Adding 'temper' can help us to control both of these factors (see page 126).

Processing the clay

Step 1

You will need to remove any unwanted material from the clay first. Natural clay might have small stones in it that will make it crack as it dries and might make enough steam to blow up the piece when it is fired. Mix your clay with water in a large container until it is thin enough to be filtered out.

Step 2

Pour your mixture through a sieve or muslin cloth and leave the larger particles behind.

Step 3

Once the clay is clean, you need to get rid of most of that water. If you leave the container out for a day or two, the clay will settle to the bottom, leaving a top layer of water that you can carefully pour off. You can strain the water through an old bedsheet.

Step 4

You will need to let this clay dry out for a day or two; you can't use it if it is too wet and slipping through your fingers.

Adding temper experiment

If you buy clay from a shop, temper has already been added. If you want to use clay that you have found in the ground you will need to experiment with adding your own temper. How much to add is tricky to gauge, as each clay is different. The goal is to find the correct amount of temper for the clay with which you are working.

Some clays will work with no temper; others will require a fairly large amount. If you add too little, the pot may crack while drying or firing; if you add too much, the clay may become crumbly and not hold together well in construction or use.

Step 1

For the purpose of this experiment, I would recommend using coarse sand or well-ground-up shells or brick as your temper. Use a pestle and mortar to grind them up.

Step 2

Take a handful of processed clay and divide it into ten small, equal-sized pieces. Make each piece into a ball and then flatten it.

Step 3

For the first experiment, cover one of your flattened balls with the temper, then combine the ten balls back together to make one complete ball again. This is your 10% temper trial. Mark this ball with one little dot using a stick.

Step 4

Now do the same again with a fresh handful of clay. This time, after covering the first disc of clay with the temper, add another disc on top and cover with temper before joining all your pieces back together again. This is your 20% temper trial. Mark this ball with two little dots using a stick. Carry on doing this until you reach 50%. That would entail covering five discs before joining them all together again into one big ball and adding five little dots with a stick.

Tip
The more often my pot will be subjected to temperature changes, especially for cooking, the more temper I add.

Materials to use for temper
Temper can be made from aquarium gravel crushed down to an appropriate size, crushed shells, old broken pottery pulverized into little pieces, or sometimes even coarse sand. The general rule is that temper should be 'edgy', not soft, so that the clay can stick into it.

Whatever you use, ensure that your temper is ground down to the same size and is made from the same material, added carefully in proportions such as 10% or 15%.

Firing the tempered clay balls

Firing can be a complicated process, but is necessary to remove all the water to make the clay hard and strong. This process is only to make clay for experimental needs, not if you want to make yourself a full clay dinner set.

AGE 8+
TIME 3+ hours
MATERIALS Large fire, heatproof gloves

Make a large fire. Each ball of clay will need to sit about 12in (30cm) away from the fire, warming and drying. You will need to keep turning the balls to make sure they dry evenly. Gradually, as they dry, move them closer and closer to the fire. After an hour or so of drying you should be able to build your fire up so that the clay balls are completely covered by the fire. Keep these balls in the fire for another hour or more, getting as hot as possible. When your fire dies down and cools, you can use a stick to roll out your balls and see which ones have survived the best.

Making a coil pot

If you are working with clay for the first time, I would recommend using air-dry clay. I have spent hours, even days, making a pot only to have it explode into smithereens during the final firing process. Air-dry clay requires no temper adding or firing.

AGE 7+
TIME 1 hour+
TOOLS Water, sponge, sticks, feathers/comb to make patterns, hard surface such as a chopping board
MATERIALS Air-dry clay

Tip
If you leave the pot to dry for around 10–15 minutes after every two to three layers of coils, it is easier to build on, as the clay starts to harden slightly. Add a little water to help join your pieces together.

Step 1

To make the base of your coil pot, take a ball of clay about the size of a ping-pong ball. Flatten the ball with the palm of your hand. Insert your thumb into the centre to make an indent and thin out the walls with your thumb and forefinger. It should now look like a small dish or saucer.

Step 2

Take another piece of clay about the same size as the first. Roll it out on a hard surface to make an even-sized 'worm' to use as your first coil. Slightly moisten the rim of the pot base (the first piece). Do not make it too damp; this will make the pot too wet to handle and it could start to collapse. Place the coil around the edge of the base. Very carefully, smooth down the edges of the outside of the pot so you cannot see the join.

Step 3

Repeat step 2, adding the next coil on top. You can choose whether to keep the coils separate on the inside or smooth these out, too.

Step 4

Add as many coils as you like to build up the walls of your pot. When it is the desired size, take three times the amount of clay used for your first coils to make the last coil. This time, once you have rolled it out, flatten it slightly with your forefinger to make a slab around $3/8$in (1cm) thick. Adding a little water, attach it to the inside of your pot at the top, overlapping the edges. Gently press the walls into the slab so that they join tightly.

Step 5

Allow the top part of the slab to curve outwards, making the lip of the pot by gently bending it out. You can now decorate your pot using sticks, feathers, shells, etc., to make markings and indents.

1

2

3

4

5

Tip

If it has been joined well and is thick enough, once the pot is completely dry the lip made in step 5 could be used to lift the pot from a fire using a stick either side.

CAVE ART AND NATURAL PAINTS

Ancient people were drawing on the walls of caves up to 40,000 years ago. Archaeologists can only guess why, but I believe they painted these images to communicate with one another, retelling epic tales of gruelling hunts and other adventures. I also like to believe that they did it to brighten up the walls of their caves, whiling away the time as they waited for a storm to pass.

Making natural paints

Ancient people made their cave art using pigments made from charcoal, blood, mud, clays and ochres. These pigments were then made into a paint or paste with various binders, including water, vegetable juices, urine, animal fat, bone marrow, blood and egg whites. They sometimes added hide glue to their paints to make them longer-lasting and help seal them onto the cave walls.

Why not find yourself a large rock, some slate, some brown paper or even your body to experiment with natural paints. If you are going to use body paint, always check for allergies first by using a tiny bit on an arm, and keep it well away from your eyes.

Ochre paints

Ochres are natural earth pigments that contain iron oxide, creating a beautiful range of reds, oranges, yellows and browns. These can be mixed with water or with oils to create different effects. Use a shell, a rock or an old plastic pot to mix ochres with water to make a paste.

You can also make a type of oil pastel by adding animal fat to ochre pigment powder. Try adding a teaspoon of lard to your paste to recreate this effect.

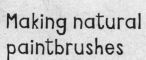

Making natural paintbrushes

Cave people applied their paints in different ways. They sometimes used sticks of charcoal, or dabbed their fingers in colours and smeared them on cave walls. They might even have made their own paintbrushes. Historians claim that brushes made from horsehair were used for paint application and outlining.

They also achieved spray effects by blowing paint through hollow bones. We have recreated this effect by using a pottery tool called an atomizer glaze pot with a little watered-down paint.

Charcoal

Charcoal can be crushed between rocks and ground down to make a powder and used either on its own as a pencil, mixed with water, or with lard or other fat.

Charcoal can be bought from art supply shops, but you can also make your own (see page 82).

Clay paints

Clays can be found in the earth or bought from a shop. Clays can make wonderful body paints. Be careful if you use clay from the earth as it could have sharp pieces of stone in it. Mix with a little water to make the clay moist enough to be applied.

Rock colours

Try breaking up soft rocks to see what colours are inside. You might find one with iron ore in the middle and use it to make reds. You can grind down large rocks to make a powder. Use your fingers to draw with the powder, or mix the powder with water or fat and turn them into paints as above.

Tip
Feathers also work really well for blending different colours together.

Willow stick paintbrushes

Try making your own paintbrushes from a stick of willow. Use a rock to pound one end which will open the fibres to create the brush.

Wild food

THERE'S NOTHING MORE DELICIOUS OR SATISFYING THAN
A MEAL SOURCED 100% FROM NATURE. WHEN YOU KNOW
WHAT TO LOOK FOR YOU'LL SOON SEE THAT AT THE RIGHT
TIME OF YEAR MOTHER NATURE PROVIDES US WITH
A FABULOUS FEAST FOR THE PICKING.

Foraged foods

Hedgerows and woodlands are great places to forage for food and medicinal plants. If you know what to look for, you can find edible plants that can be made into jams, soups, stews and cordials. Foraging for food can be both engaging and educational. There are few things more satisfying in life than bringing a basket of foraged food to the table. Learning to identify what is what, where it grows, what it looks like and which parts are edible is all part of the enjoyment.

Tip

Learn three plants inside and out. Learn their names, where they grow and which parts you can use. Go out looking for them. Draw them, pick and press them, make a fact file and create a scrapbook for each one. Get to know them as if you were getting to know a new friend. Once you are confident, get to know another three and gradually build up your knowledge.

Laws and considerations while foraging

Follow our guidelines to ensure that you forage sustainably and responsibly. This will make sure you stay safe and within the law.

- If you are not completely sure of what something is, do not pick it.

- Be aware of the law, which states that you must not dig up the roots or bulbs of a plant on public land but can pick the leaves as long as it is not for re-sale purposes and have the landowner's permission to do so.

- Even if fruit has fallen from a private fruit tree onto common land, you must still ask the owner of the tree for pernmission before you take it.

- Only take what you plan to use for yourself and only when a plant is plentiful. Take small quantities from several plants rather than stripping one bare. Plants that are left will be able to produce seeds and spores that grow into the next generation.

- Minimize damage to the nearby habitat. Take care not to trample down areas you are collecting from.

- Do not collect rare species. Only take plants when you are certain you know what they are. Take a good field guidebook to make sure you know what you are picking and avoid confusion. Some species are protected by law, so be aware of what to leave alone.

- Be aware of poisonous species and their lookalikes. Make sure you know what you are collecting before setting out if possible. Always take a guidebook with you.

Plant identification

Weed, flower or medicine, it is always good to know your plants. Foraging for herbs is a great way to get to know your local area as well as wowing your friends with your knowledge of the environment. These are my favourite plants. Get to know them well before you think about harvesting any, and always ask permission before you pick.

Dandelion

(Taraxacum)

What it is and where to find it
Dandelions are a wonder herb that most people think of as a weed. Their fluffy seed head and jagged green leaves grow in blankets in meadows and in gardens.

Herbal properties
Dandelion leaves contain vitamins A, C and K, and are good sources of calcium, potassium and iron.

Appearance
The leaves are jagged like the teeth of a lion. The seed head that grows is puffy and fluffy white and looks like a full moon. The flowers that open during the day and close by night are a vibrant yellow and orange.

Nettles

(Urtica dioica)

What it is and where to find it
Nettles can be found pretty much everywhere, in fields, woodlands and roadsides.

Herbal properties
Nettles have many healing properties including being very high in vitamin C and iron.

Appearance
The dark green, heart-shaped leaves are jagged and pointy like a giant teardrop. The stem is thick and finely haired. The flowers grow in clusters of tiny seeds hanging from the stem.

Wood sorrel

(Oxalis acetosella)

What it is and where to find it
The fresh, green, acidic-tasting leaves form distinctive clumps in woodlands and shady hedgerows, often growing from the moss on fallen logs.

Herbal properties
Sorrel is thought to have diuretic and fever-reducing properties.

Appearance
The tiny, delicate white flowers have five petals and tiny purple veins; they close as the light fades and reopen in dappled sun. Each leaf is heart-shaped and grows in a set of three.

Pot marigolds
(Calendula officinalis)

What it is and where to find it
Marigolds are part of the daisy family and loved by many gardeners for their beautiful bright yellow and orange colours.

Herbal properties
The flowers are antibacterial and antifungal, speeding up wound healing and relieving insect bites. They can also help soothe the dry hands of a woodland adventurer or gardener.

Appearance
Marigolds have vibrant orange and yellow petals. They look like mini sunflowers or bright daisies. Their leaves are long, pointy and green. Their stems are thick and green.

Cleavers
(Galium aparine)

What it is and where to find it
This plant has many names, including sticky weed, goose grass, sticky willy and grip grass. For many herbalists it has a list of health benefits longer than the list of its names.

Herbal properties
It is said to help remove trapped bacteria from the lymph glands. It is especially high in vitamin C, which helps to boost the immune system.

Appearance
Cleavers creep along with straggling stems that branch out. They attach themselves to anything in their way with small hooked hairs that grow out of the leaves and stems. The leaves are narrow and long with pointed tips and tiny gentle prickles along them. The star-shaped flowers are white with four petals. The seeds from the cleavers are little balls that stick to animals' fur. They are then dropped off elsewhere, helping the plant grow in other locations.

Wild garlic
(Allium ursinum)

What it is and where to find it
Wild garlic, also known as ramsons, is a member of the onion family. The leaves and flowers are edible. Young leaves, appearing in March, are delicious added to soups, sauces and pesto. The flowers emerge from April to June and can add a potent garlicky punch to salads. Wild garlic mainly grows in ancient woodland and on river banks.

Herbal properties
Garlic is widely known for its antibacterial qualities and contains vitamins A and C, calcium and iron. Wild garlic is thought to be effective at lowering blood pressure.

Appearance
This plant is distinguished by its strong smell. Its bright, star-like white flowers grow in vibrant clusters, often creating a blanket on the woodland floor. The leaves are long, shiny and pointy, growing in pairs.

Eating wild

I REMEMBER MY FIRST EVER REALLY WILD MEAL. I WAS INVITED TO SPEND THE
EVENING WITH FRIENDS AROUND A WOODLAND CAMPFIRE. I WAS TOLD THERE
WOULD BE FOOD FOR US ALL TO EAT. 'GREAT', I THOUGHT, 'I LOVE A GOOD DINNER
PARTY!' BUT THEN I WAS TOLD THAT THERE WOULD BE NO MODERN COOKING
EQUIPMENT USED AND NO FOOD OTHER THAN FROM NATURE.

I was nervous. I started imagining
toasted bugs presented on a giant leaf
for a starter, worm burgers served on a
woven grass mat with a side of twig chips
and a green weed salad for the main, and
a handful of berries straight from the
bush for dessert or, worse still, real mud
pies! Not my cup of tea, to say the least,
but it was too late to decline their offer;
my friends had already gone off to visit
the 'free supermarket' otherwise known
as 'the woods'.

*"I started imagining toasted bugs presented on a
giant leaf for a starter, worm burgers served on
a woven grass mat with a side of twig chips..."*

We arrived to a roaring campfire in the
middle of a ring of wooden benches. It
was a welcoming start. We were offered
a cup of tea as we arrived. I accepted,
bemused as to the lack of kettle. Instead,
large rocks were being heated in the fire.
As they began to glow red, they were
taken from the fire and swiftly plunged
into a clay pot of cold water. To my
amazement, the water took just seconds
to come to the boil! Pine needles were
added to each of our birch bark cups and
tea was served.

Our starter that evening was a bright
green nettle and sorrel soup, served
with bread made from ground nuts,
seeds, cattail roots, herbs and water and
cooked straight on the coals of the fire.
We drank from little clay pots; no need
for a spoon. The pots warmed our hands
as we drank the delicious broth, each
mouthful tasting fresh and nourishing.
I found myself excited for the next
course. No barbecued bugs in sight so far!

Our host had been fishing that evening
and caught a salmon from the river.
She heated up flat rocks on the fire, one
acting as a reflector and the other as a hot
plate, creating a sort of open oven effect.
Using her hands, she dolloped on a gloop
of buffalo fat from her gourd, which
hissed and sang as it hit the surface. She
cut a steak of salmon with a flint knife
and added that to the bubbling hot fat,
crackling and sizzling to our delight.

While the salmon was left to cook, we were each given a basket and directed to a patch of green leaves. This was a new take on a 'help yourself' buffet! We were shown how to identify the greens we were looking for and told it was a type of saxifrage that tasted like fresh spinach. We picked in the usual enthusiastic foragers' style ('one for me, one for the pot'). It was so succulent – we couldn't help ourselves!

We took what we'd collected back to the log. Morel mushrooms were added to the salmon still singing sweetly on its hot rock, and our greens were laid on top. A dollop more gloopy fat and more heated flat rocks were sandwiched on top, creating a sort of primitive 'George Forman grill' effect.

I remember wondering how much you would pay for this in a five-star restaurant. I could see it written up on the menu: 'Freshly caught river salmon, complimented with a wild mushroom tower, a sumptuous wilted

saxifrage side and a buffalo jus'. I found myself smiling; for us, no fancy words were needed: this was all free, taken and cooked straight from the earth. The whole thing was finished with

"I remember wondering how much you would pay for this in a five-star restaurant."

dessert, but not the once-feared mud pies, or a wrestle with a blackberry bush, but rather with sour berry cakes made from choke cherry and saskatoon berries dried in patties in the sun that made our tongues tingle and fizz with delight.

The whole meal was served without plates and mostly without washing up. Our planks of wood were licked clean and our clay pots washed in the river. It was mouth-wateringly delectable. I invited myself back for the next week's experience there and then, no longer scared of bug burgers and the like. Eating wild, I decided, was delicious.

Wild garlic and walnut pesto

Our daughter loves pesto and she loved the idea of foraging for wild garlic to make some. She enjoyed helping me get all the ingredients together to make it and she was excited to try it. She did not love the taste, however; it was very strong! Since that first attempt I have worked under her supervision to create the perfect balance of garlic and goodness. This is the recipe we've come up with.

AGE Any
TIME 5 minutes preparation, plus foraging time
TOOLS Food blender, storage pots

Collecting wild garlic

Wild garlic (*Allium ursinum*) grows across the UK from late winter until the end of spring. The leaves can be eaten raw or cooked. If you're walking through countryside where wild garlic grows, the garlicky scent is hard to miss. Foraging for wild garlic is a great way to get kids to engage all of their senses when out on a walk.

Ingredients

5 leaves of wild garlic
Small bunch of mint
Small bunch of basil
Handful of walnuts
1¾oz (50g) Parmesan cheese
Pinch of salt
Pinch of pepper
Good glug of olive oil
Juice of half a lemon

Step 1

Find a patch of wild garlic and pick a small bunch.

Step 2

Wash your garlic and put in a food blender. Add the rest of your ingredients and blend.

Step 3

Taste test and season to your liking, adding more salt or pepper as desired.

Step 4

Empty the contents into pots with lids and store in the fridge. This will keep for up to five days. It is great with pasta, added to roast vegetables and as a delicious alternative for a pizza base sauce.

Pickled wild garlic bulbs

If you have wild garlic growing in your garden, in nearby woodland or on a local friendly farmer's land, you might be able to make some of these pickled treats. These little gems are great in salads, with cheese and crackers or just as a snack. Remember, it is illegal to dig up the roots unless you have permission from the landowner first.

Ingredients
5oz (150g) wild garlic bulbs (trimmed and cleaned)
3½oz (100ml) white wine vinegar
¼tsp nutmeg or allspice
1tsp (5ml) yellow mustard seed
½tsp celery seeds
Small piece of fresh ginger (finely chopped)
2tbsp (35ml) of granulated sugar

This quantity makes one jar.

Step 1
Top and tail the wild garlic bulbs, and clean them thoroughly. Don't waste the leaves, though – use them for the wild garlic and walnut pesto recipe (see opposite).

Step 2
Sterilize a jam jar, and make sure the lid has a rubber seal.

Step 3
Boil up the vinegar, nutmeg or allspice, mustard and celery seeds, ginger and sugar for five minutes.

Step 4
Stuff the wild garlic bulbs into the jar, then pour over the spiced pickling vinegar. Leave in a darkened cupboard for a month or longer to develop an even deeper flavour.

AGE Any
TIME 5 minutes preparation, plus foraging time
TOOLS Food blender, storage pots

Identifying wild garlic
Wild garlic looks similar to lily of the valley and lords and ladies, both of which are poisonous. The key difference is that wild garlic always smells of garlic, but do not let this be your only point of identification. If you rub your fingers on the plant to test for the tell-tale garlic smell, this scent will remain on your fingers, making every plant thereafter smell of garlic. If you are in any doubt about which plant you've found, do not eat it.

Cleaver juice

This cleaver juice results in a brilliant green magic shot that helps reboot the system. The whole family drinks this juice for the whole of spring, when we sport green-tinged tongues but have very healthy bodies!

Ingredients
Handful of cleavers
Thumb-sized piece of ginger (optional)
1tsp (5ml) honey (optional)
Dash of warm water

AGE Any
TIME 15 minutes
TOOLS Pestle and mortar, sieve or square of muslin, glass

Collecting cleavers
Part of the joy of this juice is in the collecting of the plant. As a child (and, I confess, as an immature adult, too), I entertained myself on family walks by pulling up cleavers to throw at people's unsuspecting backs. The sticky buds would cling in hilarious clumps, amusing me while I congratulated myself for my ninja skills – until I realized someone had got me, too! Our five-year-old loves foraging for this sticky plant. I always come home with a bunch still hanging on my back and her laughing at my unknown organic following.

Step 1
Find a patch of fresh early-spring cleavers and pick them.

Step 2
Using a pestle and mortar, pound and grind the cleavers until they are broken up and the green juices start being released. If you are using ginger (another immune booster and anti-inflammatory), pound this up at the same time.

Step 3
Strain the juices into a glass using a square of muslin or a sieve.

Step 4
If you are using honey (yet another immune booster), stir in a teaspoon full and add a dash of hot water to make the juice a bit more palatable. Then drink!

Health benefits
Nature provides us with what we need at the right time of year. In the summer, we can grow crisp green lettuces, juicy tomatoes and cool cucumbers, satisfying our cravings for a refreshing salad on a hot day. In the colder months, we grow root vegetables, ideal for stews and casseroles to fulfill our need for comfort foods that warm us from the inside. And as the spring sun starts to shine, and our immune systems have had enough battering from the cold winter months, cleavers (*Galium aparine*) begin to show their heads.

Cleaver has many alternative names, including sticky weed, goose grass, sticky willy and grip grass. Herbalists believe the plant has as many health benefits as it has names. It is said to act on the lymphatic system, removing and draining poisons and trapped bacteria from the lymph glands. It is high in vitamin C too, which helps to combat the symptoms of the nasty common cold.

Cleaver and nettle cordial

There is so much that you can do with nettles; this cordial makes a wonderfully refreshing springtime drink. Mixed with fizzy or still water it works as an energizing and revitalizing drink as well as a way to weed the garden! This is a great way to get more apprehensive people to sample wild food and make them realize that 'wild' doesn't have to mean scary!

AGE Any
TIME 20 minutes, plus foraging time
TOOLS Saucepan, scales, salad spinner, thermometer, sieve or colander, sterile glass bottles with tops

Ingredients
3½oz (100g) 100g freshly picked young cleavers
3½oz (100g) freshly picked nettle tops
35oz (1kg) granulated sugar
1½oz (40g) citric acid
17 fluid oz (500ml) water

Step 1
Collect nettles and cleavers and wash and spin dry in a salad spinner.

Step 2
Weigh out 35oz (1kg) of granulated sugar.

Step 3
Measure out 1½oz (40g) of citric acid. Citric acid can be found in health stores or home brewing shops.

Step 4
Add the granulated sugar, citric acid and water to a large saucepan, heat the mixture until it reaches 140°F (60°C), then remove from the heat.

Step 5
Add the nettle and cleaver leaves, stir well so they are steeped in the liquid, then cover and leave for a week. Stir your cordial mixture daily.

Step 6
After a week is up, sterilize your bottles, then strain the liquid through a sieve or colander and bottle it.

My batch lasted about four weeks. After opening a bottle, make sure that you refrigerate your cordial.

Nettle tea

When I lived out in the wild there was nothing better than coming back from a hunt, snow threatening from above, hands tingly cold, cheeks rosy red, to be greeted with a clay pot of steaming tea. Our tea was always made up from whatever edible had been foraged that day. Nettle tea was one of the best teas we were blessed with.

AGE Any
TIME 10 minutes
TOOLS Saucepan to boil water in, stove top or fire

How to pick nettles, without getting stung!

Here's how to pick nettles without getting stung: nettles are covered with tiny hairs filled with irritating chemicals. When you brush against these hairs, the chemicals are released, causing the sting. Therefore, to avoid being stung, you need to touch the plant without breaking the hairs. Look for fresh leaves at the top of the plant. Pinch the leaves firmly from underneath, then twist the leaf and pluck it off with a quick, firm grasp. If you're too gentle, you might snag a hair and break it.

Ingredients
Nettles

Step 1
Find a nice juicy patch of nettles. Pick the top few young leaves; we usually allow ten nettle heads per litre of water.

Step 2
Add the nettles to a pan of water. Bring to the boil.

Step 3
Let the tea cool a little to let the flavours disperse and become cool enough to drink.

Nettle energy balls

Nettles are fabulous. Yes, they sting and seem to grow in all the wrong places, but I consider them a gift from the nature gods. Here is a sweet treat recipe to help unleash some of that goodness and nourish our bodies.

Ingredients
8oz (225g) dates

4oz (110g) soaked sunflower seeds (soak 3oz/85g of dried sunflower seeds and leave overnight, drain and rinse, then leave for a few hours to dry slightly)

6tsp (35ml) chopped raw nettle

1–2tsp (5–10ml) coconut oil

½tbsp (8ml) cocoa powder

1tsp (5ml) cinnamon (optional)

1tsp (5ml) dried nori flakes (optional – this gives a strong and unique taste but adds iron)

2tsp (10ml) desiccated coconut

For the topping: 1tbsp (15ml) desiccated coconut

AGE Any
TIME 10 minutes, plus foraging time
TOOLS Food blender, plate, airtight container for storage

Health benefits
Studies have shown that stinging nettles have antioxidant, antimicrobial, anti-ulcer, astringent and analgesic capabilities. Combine this with their high level of vitamin C and, used in the appropriate ways, they can help heal ailments including hayfever, urinary issues and joint pain. They can also reduce bleeding and help ease eczema.

IMPORTANT Put the nettle tops and leaves in a food processor with an S-blade and chop very finely. The result should look like finely chopped parsley. The nettles won't sting once they have been chopped.

Step 1
Pick the nettles. Use gloves if you are concerned about getting stung. If you don't have gloves, use your thumb and forefinger and pinch from under the leaves and pull up. You only want to pick the top fresh 'new' leaves. Remember: only pick what you need. (If you pick too many leaves, steep them in boiling water to make a herbal tea – see opposite.)

Step 2
Blend the soaked sunflower seeds and the chopped raw nettles in a food processor with an S-blade until roughly chopped.

Step 3
Add the remaining ingredients to the food processor and blend again until the mixture resembles fine crumbs.

Step 4
Take small scoops of the mixture and roll them into balls using the palms of your hands.

Step 5
Roll each ball in desiccated coconut. Put them into the refrigerator for an hour or so, or as long as it takes for them to firm up. Once they are firm, store in an airtight container.

AGE 7+
TIME 2 days
TOOLS Saucepan, scissors, sieve, spoon, small bowl, pot to store it in
MATERIALS Kitchen towel

Dandelion syrup

This is a delicious way to use up a common garden weed. Dandelions have lots to offer: they are high in vitamin C, iron and potassium and they make a super sweet, tasty syrup that can be drizzled over ice-cream or yoghurt — or mixed with water or fizzy water to make a refreshing drink.

Ingredients
100 dandelion flower heads
2 cups of sugar
1 lemon
water

Step 1
Pick your flowers. Wash them, cut the petals off and put them to dry on a kitchen towel.

Step 2
When dry, put the petals in a pot and cover them with water. Bring them to a rolling boil for about one minute. Remove from the heat and cover. When cool, put in the fridge to steep overnight.

Step 3
The next morning, use a sieve to strain the petals from the water over a bowl, pressing the petals with a spoon to extract as much juice as possible. Return the strained water to the pot, add the sugar and lemon juice and simmer, covered, on low heat until it has thickened, stirring occasionally. The more sugar you use, the thicker the end result. Check the consistency after an hour. Dip a spoon into the syrup, let it cool and test it with your finger. If it is thick enough it will stick to the back of the spoon.

Step 4
Store in the fridge for up to three weeks. Drizzle over ice cream or yoghurt, or mix with water as a drink.

Fruit leathers

This is a great way to use up any excess fruit come apple season or blackberry picking time and can be kept for months if kept in an airtight well-sealed container. Great for lunch boxes and healthy snacks.

Ingredients
4 cups berries/chopped fruit of choice
2–4tbsp (35–70ml) honey
1tbsp (17.5ml) lemon juice
2–4tbsp (35–70ml) of water (as needed)

Four cups of fruit yields about one baking sheet of fruit leather

Step 1
Add the fruit, honey, lemon juice, and water (if needed) to your pan. Cover with a lid. Cook on a low heat until the fruit release its juices and combines together. Let the mixture cook down until thickened.

Step 2
Add the cooled fruit to your blender or food processor and blend until very smooth. Strain through a sieve to remove seeds if you are using berries.

Step 3
Spread the thick fruit puree onto a baking sheet, using a spatula to get a nice, even surface. This is important, so that it dries evenly.

Step 4
Bake at 210°F (100°C) in the oven, leaving the door partly open. Cook for around three hours depending on thickness. Sometimes one section will dry faster, so you might need to turn the tray occasionally.

Step 5
The fruit leather is done when it is tacky but not sticky, and it should not be hard. Peel back the edges; if it does not stick, it is probably done. Some fruits turn out more 'leathery' or chewy than others. Just experiment to find your favourite combination. Roll in cling film and twist the ends to seal.

AGE 5+
TIME 30+ minutes
TOOLS Saucepan, non-stick baking sheet, metal baking sheet, cling film, food processor or hand blender, spatula

Variations
Try adding carrots or other vegetables to your fruit. Add spices like ginger for a kick.

Baked apples

This is a lovely simple recipe, great for any time of the year. In late summer and during autumn you can forage for your own apples from trees and hedgerows. Even windfalls are good; once cooked, you won't notice the odd bruise — in fact, they will just add to the sweetness. Add cream, custard, ice cream or crème fraîche, and you will have a delicious dessert in about ten minutes.

AGE 5+
TIME 10+ minutes
TOOLS Mixing bowl, spoon, foil, apple corer, chopping board, knife

Variations

Try this method with an ice-cream cone instead. Stuff with marshmallows, chocolate buttons, biscuits, berries... whatever your heart desires. Wrap in foil and put in the coals, just like the apples. Leave for about 5–10 minutes and eat when cool.

Ingredients

4 apples
handful of raisins
1tsp (5ml) of cinnamon
2tbsp (35ml) brown sugar

Step 1

Light a fire. Core your apples using an apple corer. Cut the end of each core (about ¾in/2cm) and put aside, then discard the rest. This part of the core will act as a plug later on.

Step 2

Mix together the raisins, sugar and cinnamon in a bowl.

Step 3

Insert a piece of core that you kept from Step 1 into one end of each apple, like a small plug.

Step 4

Fill your apple with the sugar mix and wrap completely in foil.

Step 5

Nestle these into the coals of your fire for about 20 minutes. By this time your apples should be soft and oozing caramel mix.

Step 6

Wait until cool enough to eat. These are gorgeous with custard or cream if you fancy adding to the treat!

Toffee apples

Everyone loves toffee apples, but for some reason they're usually only available around October for Halloween. Below is a simple recipe so you can create this sweet treat whenever you like. Be careful though; it's a dangerous skill to have. A toffee apple a day may keep the dentist in pay (or something like that!).

Ingredients
Apples
Brown sugar
Cinnamon (optional)

Step 1
Peel your apple.

Step 2
Sharpen one end of your stick.

Step 3
Mix up a handful of brown sugar with a sprinkling of cinnamon and keep to one side.

Step 4
Skewer your apple on the sharp end of your stick. Cook over your fire, turning frequently. It's ready when it starts to bubble all over.

Step 5
Be careful, as it's hot now! Roll in your sugar mix until completely covered.

Step 6
Cook on the fire again, rotating frequently until all the sugar has completely melted.

Step 7
Wait until the toffee has cooled and then eat.

AGE 7+
TIME 15–20 minutes
MATERIALS A stick

Bare-hands cooking

Bare-hands cooking is our way of describing what we call 'smart cooking'. It needs limited pots and pans and makes good use of the natural materials that can be found around us. Here are some simple yet delicious ways to prepare food where the only washing up will be a few mixing bowls. Occasionally you even get to eat your saucepan and compost your pots and pans. Simply lick your fingers and the cleaning up is done. It couldn't be more satisfying!

AGE 7+
TIME 2 hours
TOOLS Knife, chopping board, string, cup of water, split hazel stick 3ft (1m) long, 3 hazel sticks for skewers, fire

Tip

Cooking the chicken will need a well-maintained fire with good hot coals. If you don't have a good wood source, cooking over a bag of barbecue coals works well, too, but you'll need to keep your fire well stocked to make sure it's hot enough to cook on.

Spatchcock chicken

Spatchcocking is a technique used for preparing poultry or game birds for roasting or grilling. It involves removing the backbone and other bones to flatten out the meat before cooking; this is also known as 'butterflying' the bird. This allows the meat to cook evenly and thoroughly over the fire.

Ingredients
One chicken

Preparation
Split a 3ft (1m) hazel stick the length of your chicken, plus a half (see page 101). You'll also need three smaller hazel twigs pointed at both ends and some string soaked in water.

Step 1
Lay the chicken breast side down.

Step 2
Feel for the spine by running your finger along the back of the chicken.

Step 3
Place the tip of the knife vertically to one side of the spine and press firmly, cutting through the bone.

Step 4
Repeat on the opposite side.

Step 5
Remove the spine and the chicken should fall open.

Step 6
Cut off the wing tips.

Step 7
Place the chicken in the split stick and tie the ends of the stick together.

Step 8
Pierce the meat with the skewers. Make a hole in the ground then place the hazel stick into it, angled over the hot coals. Cook for 90 minutes to 2 hours or until the juices run clear.

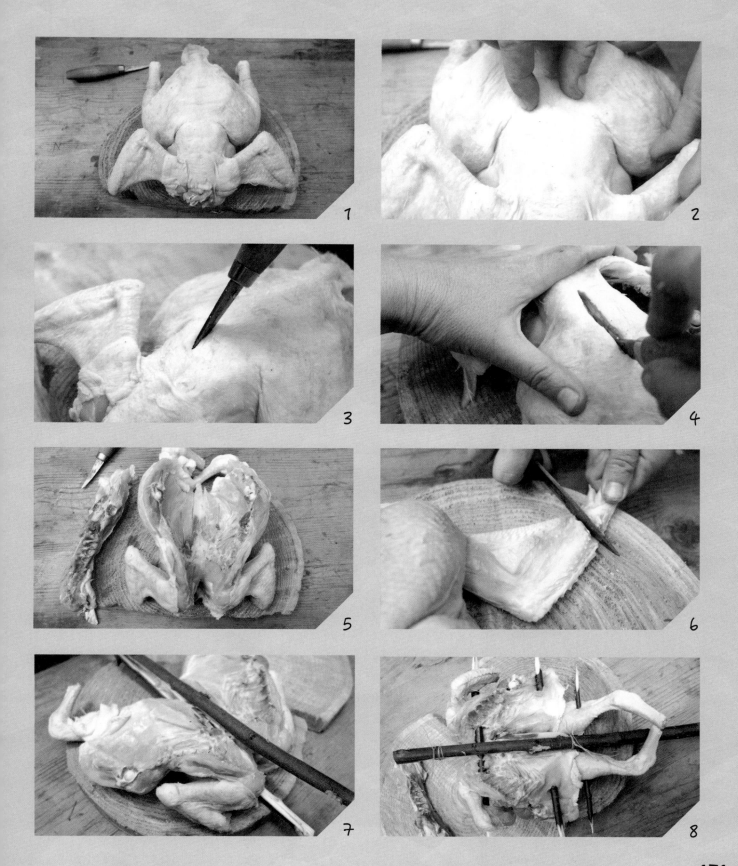

AGE 10+
TIME 30 minutes
TOOLS Hazel pole, hazel sticks, knife, string, roaring fire, chopping board
KNOTS Clove hitch (see page 51)

Ponassed trout

Ponassing is probably one of the best ways to eat fish. This technique involves removing the head, bones and tail, leaving one complete fillet, which is then suspended over the fire using a stick framework. It's a great way of making sure the fish cooks evenly and all the way through.

Ingredients
A whole trout

Preparation
You'll need to find a long, fresh hazel stick, twice the length of your fish and about 2ft (60cm) more. This stick will need to be split the length of your fish. To safely split it, refer to the knife cutting techniques (see page 101). You'll also need at least three smaller hazel twigs, pointed at both ends. Lastly, you'll need some string or cordage, preferably soaked in water so that it won't burn on contact with the fire. You will also need a brilliantly blazing fire.

Step 1
Cut the trout down to the spine around the head, cutting from behind the gills. Leave the head attached, though; you're only cutting to the bone, not through the bone. Do the

same with the tail. Cut out the top fin and cartilage there. Leave the side fins on for now.

Step 2
Cut along the bottom so that you can open up your fish to reach the spine and ribs. Lever them out by running your fingers down either side of the spine to work it away from the flesh. You should be able to remove it in one piece, just like a cartoon fish skeleton!

Step 3
Place your fish between the two prongs of your big split stick. Here's where your smaller pointy sticks come in. Pierce the flesh side and push the skewer through the back of the fish and through the holding stick and pierce the other side to hold open the fish.

1

2

3

4

5

Step 4
Use your wet string to tie the stick ends together so that your fish is nice and tight in place.

Step 5
Lastly, dig the other end of the stick in the ground so that the fish is angled over the fire. The general rule is that if you can hold your hand, where your fish is, over the fire for longer than eight seconds it won't be hot enough to cook your fish; you'll need to bring the fish in a little closer. The flesh will start to turn in colour and become harder and less squishy. Then you know that it's cooked. No seasoning is needed, and there's no washing up.

Planked trout
This is a fun alternative way to cook fish around the fire and is a traditional method of cooking in Finland. The wood you use leaves a bit of its flavour with the fish after it is cooked, adding to this mouthwatering dish.

Drill holes every 1in (2.5cm) along the top and bottom edges of a plank of cedar (birch, maple, alder, oak and beech work too). Use sharpened twigs to peg the gutted fish onto the plank. Place the plank next to your fire, making sure the plank is slightly angled away. Cook for about 10–15 minutes.

COOKING INSIDE FRUIT AND VEGETABLES

In these fun recipes, fruit and vegetables become your pots and pans, making the need for modern equipment very limited. Cooking food nestled into the hot coals of a fire is one of life's simple pleasures and you can sit back and relax in the warmth while the food is cooking.

Orange couscous

This is a scrummy way to cook couscous that is beautifully fluffy and orange flavoured! It tastes yummy with the ponassed trout on page 152. When you have finished, keep the scooped-out orange and use it for the recipes on pages 156 and 157.

AGE Any
TIME 10 minutes
TOOLS Knife, chopping board, fire

Ingredients
An orange
Packet of couscous

Step 1
Cut off the top of a large navel orange and set it aside. Scoop out the flesh of the orange and enjoy the juicy insides.

Step 2
Pour in the dry couscous, filling the skin about a quarter of the way.

Step 3
Pour freshly boiled water over the couscous so it is just covered, plus ³/₈in (1cm) more. Put the 'lid' back on and wait 5–10 minutes for the couscous to soften and cook.

AGE Any
TIME 20 minutes
TOOLS Knife, chopping board, fire

Egg in a pepper

This is a fun and different way to cook an egg that will impress your friends around the campfire. You can even eat your saucepan afterwards! When else can you do that?

Ingredients
One pepper
One egg

Step 1
Cut the top off a pepper and place it aside.

Step 2
Crack an egg into the pepper. (Do not attempt to break the egg on the side of the pepper – it does not work and people will laugh!)

Step 3
Place the 'lid' back on your pepper. Nestle the pepper and egg into the coals of your fire and leave to cook. You might want to stir the egg with a stick halfway through to rotate the hot bits from the side.

Lemon cake in a lemon

Add this simple and easy way to make a lemon cake to your campfire repertoire. Sit back and enjoy with a campfire brew. On hot days, why not also make a delicious and tart homemade lemonade? Keep the lemon juice and flesh that you scoop out and mix them up with 1tsp of sugar and some fizzy water.

Ingredients
1 lemon
2oz (50g) butter
2oz (50g) sugar
2oz (50g) self-raising flour
1 egg

AGE Any
TIME 25 minutes
TOOLS Knife, mixing bowl, spoon, fire, tin foil

Step 1
Cut the top off the lemon and set it aside. Squeeze out the juice from the 'lid', then scoop out the lemon juice and flesh from the main part.

Step 2
Make up a lemon cake mix. You can use a ready-made mix, or make one from scratch using equal amounts of butter, sugar and flour (2oz/50g of each should make about six cakes), then add an egg and some lemon zest.

Step 3
Fill the lemon halfway with the cake mix. Do not over-fill it unless you want to end up with a messy exploding soufflé. Place the 'lid' back on and wrap the entire thing in tin foil, making a giant foil bauble. Twist to close at the top, making it safer and easier to take out of the fire. Nestle it in the coals for about 20 minutes until cooked through.

Tip
If you can hold your hand over the coals for more than five seconds comfortably, your fire is not hot enough to cook on and will need stoking.

Variation
Choolate and orange are a great combination. Try a chocolate cake mix in an orange by making the basic cake mix in step 2. Instead of adding lemon zest, replace a bit of the flour with cocoa powder. Fill and cook in the same way as the lemon cake above.

Cinnamon rolls in an orange

These delicious rolls use orange not only as a flavour, but as a saucepan too! Eat them up as a perfect pudding to finish off a bare-hands, back-to-basics meal.

AGE Any
TIME 15 minutes
TOOLS Knife, chopping board, fire, tin foil

Ingredients
One cup of self-raising flour
Half a cup of raisins
2tsp (10ml) cinnamon
2tbsp (30ml) brown sugar
Water
One orange

Step 1
Make up your batter. Mix together the flour with the raisins, 1tbsp (15ml) of brown sugar and 2tbsp (30ml) of water. Mix into a stiff dough.

Step 2
Separately, mix together 1tbsp (15ml) of brown sugar, 2tsp (10ml) of cinnamon and a dash of water into a paste.

Step 3
Roll out your dough into a long sausage. Flatten to around ³/₈in (1cm) thick and about 8in (20cm) long. Spread a thick layer of your sugar paste over this. Coil your dough up to make a type of wagon wheel. Make it big enough so that it will sit in the bottom of your orange, then flatten it. You want it to be about ³/₈in (1cm) thick again at this point.

Step 4
Cut off the top of an orange. Scoop out the fleshy insides and eat them. Place your wagon wheel in the bottom of the orange. Put a foil lid on top and nestle the whole thing into the coals of your fire. Cook for 15–20 minutes.

BREAD

Do you have any idea how tasty flour and water can be? Well, it can be absolutely delicious if done in the right way. All of these recipes are best cooked on an open fire. You will need a good bed of coals to cook your ash breads on, so make the fire in advance of making your dough. You can make these breads gluten free by substituting with a gluten-free flour.

AGE Any
TIME 20 minutes
TOOLS Mixing bowl, knife, tongs, fir, tin foil

Variations
Try a savoury alternative by taking out the sugar, apple and cinnamon and adding small chunks of feta or goat's cheese, and slices of sundried tomatoes and herbs. Roll in a little salt and pepper.

Poppity ping doughnut balls

Apparently, poppity ping is Welsh slang for 'microwave' but these treats have nothing to do with a microwave. In our family we have always called any food that you can pop into your mouth in one a poppity ping; we have no idea why!

Ingredients
Sunflower oil
One chopped apple
1tsp (5ml) cinnamon
6oz (175g) self-raising flour
1tbsp (15ml) brown sugar for the main mix, and 1tbsp (15ml) to coat the balls afterwards

Step 1
Chop your apples up finely into tiny chunks. Mix in the cinnamon, 1tbsp (15ml) of brown sugar, and the flour. Add a dash of water and mix gently. You do not want a firm dough for this but a sticky one. Be careful not to mix the dough too much, so the insides are fluffy when cooked.

Step 2
Pour oil into a pan to a depth of $^3/_8$in (1cm) and heat. Drop small spoonfuls of your mixture into the oil and turn using a spoon as soon as they start to turn brown. They will cook very quickly if the oil is hot enough, but will spit and burn if it is too hot. If the oil is spitting, take it off the heat and wait a moment until it calms down..

Step 3
Once the balls are cooked, take off the heat and drop them into a bowl of brown sugar. Coat them all over with the sugar and eat. They are like mini-doughnuts and completely irresistible!

FOREST SCHOOL ADVENTURE

Ash breads

This recipe is very simple. People have been making bread in this way for hundreds of years. The ingredients given are only a guide; you can add whatever you want to your mixture.

AGE 4+
TIME 10+ minutes
TOOLS Tongs, mixing bowl, spoon

Ingredients
6oz (175g) self-raising flour
A few splashes of water

Step 1
Mix together the flour with a few splashes of water. Too much water and your dough will be too gooey; too little and you will end up with breadcrumbs. Keep adding flour and water until you get the right mix. Use your hands to squidge the dough together. You want to end up with dough that holds together but does not stick to your hands.

Step 2
Now break the dough up into pieces the size of ping-pong balls and squash them between the palms of your hands. Place them directly onto the coals of your fire. If the coals are nice and hot your bread should cook in just a minute each side. Keep turning until golden on each side (don't worry if they burn a little; this just adds to the flavour). Check that they are cooked all the way through by breaking one open. If it is still gooey it needs a little longer and perhaps more wood on your fire to bring the heat back up. Eat with lashings of chocolate spread for a really gooey delicious treat!

Cheesy bread twists
Make the same dough as for the ash bread, adding some grated cheese. Break it into pieces the size of tennis balls. Using your hands, squish the dough into long sausages. Twist it around the end of a green stick approximately 39in (1m) long, hazel or sycamore work well. Hold the stick next to the fire for 10–15 minutes, while your bread cooks. Keep turning it so it turns golden-brown all around. When it is cooked it will sound hollow when you tap it. You can eat it as it is or stuffed with butter and extra cheese.

Games

YOU DON'T NEED LOTS OF EQUIPMENT TO HAVE FUN
OUTSIDE. JUST A FEW IDEAS, SOME SIMPLE RULES,
WILLINGNESS TO BE A BIT SILLY AND WIDE OPEN SPACE.
GAMES ARE GREAT WAYS FOR CHILDREN TO EXERCISE
AND BOND TOGETHER IN A SHARED EXPERIENCE.

Warm-up games

These games are excellent ways for children to start moving their bodies, get their senses tuned in and get in touch with the environment – as well as being a perfect excuse to be silly and have some fun.

Head up head down

AGE 3+
RESOURCES None
PLAYERS Minimum 6
DURATION 5+ minutes

Stand in a circle facing each other. A 'caller' is allocated. This person does not play. The caller instructs everyone to look down to the ground. When the caller is ready, they will say 'Look up'. The players must choose a person in the circle to look directly at. If they are looking back, both are then out. If they are looking at someone else, they continue to play again.

Ninja stick

AGE 4+
RESOURCES
One stick per pair
PLAYERS 2+
DURATION
5+ minutes

Each pair has a stick. Between them they must decide who is the 'dropper' and who is the 'catcher'. The catcher will place a flat palm above the stick but not touching it. On the count of three, the dropper will drop the stick and the catcher has to try to catch it.

VARIATION Get the catcher to wear a blindfold.

Put your coat on

Before the game starts, allocate a 'rabbit'. This person will stand at least ten paces away from the group with their back turned. The group members are the 'hunters'. All of the coats and hats will be scattered between the hunters' starting line and the rabbit. Rabbits are very sensitive to noise and movement, therefore the hunters must creep up on them without being seen moving. The only problem is that it is bad weather and each hunter must be wearing a coat and hat if they wish to capture the rabbit. The hunters may steal coats and hats from others but must not be seen moving if the rabbit turns around. The rabbit can turn without warning, choose anyone that is moving and send them back to the beginning, taking off their coats or hats. The first one to get to the rabbit in full outdoor gear wins.

VARIATION Add in more or fewer coats and hats. Add in gloves and scarves, too.

AGE 5+
RESOURCES
At least as many coats or hats as there are players
PLAYERS 3+
DURATION
10+ minutes

Seven-second camouflage

AGE 5+
RESOURCES
Camouflage outfit
PLAYERS 4
minimum, but the
more the merrier

Get one person to put on their camouflage outfit. This could be a homemade ghillie suit, woollen jumper, camouflage material clothes or even just some well-placed leaves and a muddy face.

The aim is for the camouflaged candidate to conceal themselves from the rest of the group in seven seconds. Remember, leaping onto the woodland floor and using the surrounding environment as concealment is more skilled than hiding behind a large tree.

The leader shouts 'Go!' The group huddles around with their heads down and eyes closed, counting together loudly and slowly. When the time is up, the leader will be the only one who can move. If anyone in the group thinks they know where the person is, they can direct the leader, but must not move themselves.

I've played this game where the most skilled and tactical player had been less than a metre away and not been found until they've jumped out and scared us out of our wits!

VARIATION Get more than one person hiding at a time.

Tip
Try cutting up woollen blankets to make a simple waistcoat for a natural camouflage outfit. You can make holes in the material, cut strands off the edges and tie them on. Woollen jumpers in greens and browns from a charity shop could also be used.

Team games and energizers

These games are designed to foster a sense of teamwork, cooperation and community, while releasing plenty of silliness. Little equipment is needed, just an openness to communicate, work together and, above all, have fun.

Blind fetch

AGE 8+
RESOURCES Colourful cups, waymarkers or sticks – as many items as there are people in a team. Blindfolds for as many as there are teams
PLAYERS 6+
DURATION 10+ minutes

Teams of at least three are created. Each team discusses the order in which they will race. The chosen items are placed at least 20 paces away. Each set of items will be opposite each individual team. On 'go', the first player in each team puts on a blindfold. The rest of the team must direct their blindfolded player to collect the first of their items and bring them back, still blindfolded. The team must not move, though, and stay behind the start line only using their voices to direct their team member. The winners are the first team that successfully brings back each of their items. On completion, the winning team must sit down and sing 'row, row, row your boat' loudly while doing a rowing motion to indicate that they have won. Play continues until the last team is home.

VARIATION For older groups, use items of various sizes that could be used in a survival scenario (an item of clothing, a bar of chocolate, a match, etc.) and instruct the teams that they have to bring them back in the correct order. A match is hard to find in grass, but it is hilarious to watch people trying!

Tail grab

AGE 4+
RESOURCES Strips of fabric to make tails
PLAYERS 6+
DURATION 5+ minutes

Each player has a tail tucked into the back of their trousers. The leader shouts 'go' and tells them to move around in a certain manner. For example, 'walk like you're on the moon' or 'Move around like you're sneaking downstairs to get the last piece of chocolate cake out of the fridge'. When the leader chooses, they shout 'tail grab' and counts down from 10 loudly. During that time, all players must try to steal a tail from another player. If a player has their tail taken they are out unless they can grab another tail within the ten seconds. The winner is the one left with their tail.

VARIATIONS Extend the time to allow for more tail stealing.

Giant rock paper scissors

AGE 3+
RESOURCES None
PLAYERS 6+
DURATION 2+ minutes

Explain the basic rules of the game rock, paper, scissors: rock beats scissors by blunting them; scissors beat paper by cutting it, and paper beats rock by wrapping around it. The group is shown how to create each tool with their body. Scissors are made from outstretched clapping hands, rock is made by squatting on the ground, head covered, in a ball-like shape, and paper is made by arms stretched above the head. The group is divided in two. The teams go away and decide collectively which of the three they are going

to be. When the teams have decided, they stand facing one another and on the count of three they become their chosen tool. The winning team gets to choose a member from the opposing team. Alternatively, you can play with a point system – first to five, for example.

VARIATION Change rock, paper, scissors to giants, wizards, dwarfs, with appropriate actions to go along with them. Giants squash dwarfs; dwarfs tickle the feet of wizards; wizards cast a spell on giants.

Longest line

AGE 5+
RESOURCES Only what you have on your body
PLAYERS 10+
DURATION 5+ minutes

Divide the group into two. Each team begins from the same start line. They have one minute to form the longest unbroken line. They can use their own bodies and anything on their body including clothes, but instruct them to keep their underwear on (you'd be surprised!). When the time is up, the lines will need to be judged. The winning team is the one with the longest continuous line.

VARIATIONS Vary the amount of time allowed depending on group size and age.

Hunt the humless

All players are on all fours with blindfolds on, humming loudly and crawling around. The leader does not play. They explain to the group that one person will be chosen by being touched on the head. If this happens, they stop humming, stop moving, take off their blindfold and become silent. They are the 'humless'. The aim is for the rest of the group to try to find the humless by moving around and humming at one another. If the person hums back, they know they need to keep hunting. If the person does not hum back, they have found the humless. At this point, they can attach themselves to the humless, stop humming, take off their blindfold and silently watch the rest of the group crawling around humming!

VARIATION If it's too difficult due to rough terrain, this game can be played standing up in the same way; the players must move slowly and be monitored closely by others.

AGE 5+
RESOURCES A clear safe area, blindfolds
PLAYERS 6+
DURATION 10+ minutes

Stick tower

AGE 3+
RESOURCES Sticks
PLAYERS Any
DURATION 5–15 minutes

This game can be played with individuals or as a group. Each individual or team is given 14 sticks of the same size. They are given a designated time between 5 and 15 minutes to build the tallest freestanding tower or structure with their sticks.

VARIATION Alter the amount of time given and the size and number of sticks.

Helium stick

AGE 7+
RESOURCES A bamboo cane or straight hazel stick, at least 5ft (1.5m) long
PLAYERS 5+
DURATION 5+ minutes

Explain that the stick is magical and is full of helium. The challenge is for the group to lower the stick to the ground. The group is divided into two lines facing one another with their index fingers pointing across to the person opposite. The stick is balanced on top of the outstretched index fingers. Explain that once the stick is touching their finger they must not lose contact with the stick and must remain straight. They should work as a team to try to lower the stick. They will be surprised to see that the stick wants to float upwards.

VARIATION Try this with eyes closed.

Egg drop

AGE 4+
RESOURCES An egg, natural materials available such as grasses, sticks, leaves, etc.
PLAYERS Any
DURATION 5+ minutes

This challenge can be done as individuals or in groups. The aim is to create a nest for an egg that will be tested by dropping it. Get the team to think about the way a bird's nest is created and use any natural materials around; for example, weaving grasses. After an agreed amount of time, test the nests by dropping them from as a high a height as possible – preferably at least 6ft (2m) – that is safe to get to.

Egg catapult

AGE 7+
RESOURCES Per group: Metal spoon, 10 elastic bands, 10 sticks, bamboo pole, egg
PLAYERS Any
DURATION 5+ minutes

The aim is for the team to use their items to make a catapult. They do not have to use all their materials but cannot use anything additional. At the end of the designated time, test the catapults and measure the distance the egg travels.

VARIATION Allow more or fewer materials to be used.

Resources

Books

Ray Mears Bushcraft, Coronet Books, 2004

How to connect with Nature
by Tristan Gooley, Macmillan, 2014

I love my World by Chris Holland,
Wholeland, 2014

Coyote's Guide to Connecting with Nature by
Jon Young, Evan McGown and Ellen Haas,
Owlink Media, 2010

Collins Complete Guide to British Trees by Paul
Sterry, Collins, 2008

*National Wildlife Federation Field Guide to
Trees of North America* by Bruce Kershner,
Sterling, 2008

Websites

www.forestschoolassociation.org

www.outback2basics.co.uk

Magazines

Bushcraft & Survival Skills

About the authors

Dan Westall and Naomi Walmsley run Outback2Basics from their patch of woodland in Shropshire, UK. Specializing in bushcraft and Stone Age skills, they provide unique experiences for school children and teachers to connect to nature. Dan has been a bushcraft teacher for many years and has also acted as a medic and survival consultant on various TV shows. Naomi is a qualified bushcraft instructor and Forest School Leader and has also written about bushcraft and parenting for many magazines, including *Bushcraft & Survival Skills, Living Woods* and *Juno.* Together, they undertook a five-month Stone Age immersion experience in the US, living in the wilderness without any modern equipment, profoundly influencing their lives and teaching.

www.outback2basics.co.uk

Acknowledgements

To all the children who posed, jumped, ran, ate, hid, created, stalked, sneaked and played in the woods while we took photos. A giant, wild thank you.

To Naomi's parents for supporting, editing and looking after the bushcraft babes while we wrote and played (I mean worked) in the woods.

Thank you to Christian Rwirangira for all his creative input and for teaching us how to boil an egg on an open fire, in a plastic bag.

To our wonderfully helpful daughter, Maggie, who put up with us ordering her around for various photographs for the book, instead of climbing trees.

Picture credits

All photos by Dan Westall and Rachel Walmsley, except the following from Shutterstock.com: page 43 (middle) Patio; page 43 (bottom) Oksana Mizina, page 42 (bottom left) Petr Pe, page 74 (top left) Andrii Zhezhera, page 74 (top right) Imladris, page 75 (bottom) JohnatAPW, page 76 (top and middle) komkrit Preechachanwate, page 76 (bottom) colin robert varndell, page 77 (middle left) nuchstockphoto, page 77 (middle right) waldru, page 77 (bottom right) Colby A Lysne, page 92 (bottom) N_Sakarin, page 93 (top) kzww, page 110 (left) nnattalli, page 110 (middle) Africa Studio, page 110 (right) Emilio100, page 126 Maryna Pleshkun, page 130 (top) gerasimov_foto_174, page 134 Dezajny, page 135 Jacqui Martin, page 136 (left) and page 146 (right) Lubava, page 136 (right) gualtiero boffi, page 137 (right) liveostockimages, page 141 (top) Ivan Marjanovic, page 141 (bottom) jkelly, page 143 (top right) Volodymyr Nikitenko, page 144 (bottom) Madeleine Steinbach, page 147 (bottom left) andrewtit, page 147 (bottom right) Alter-ego and page 152 (top left) Piotr Wawrzyniuk.
Illustration on inside cover by Rebecca Mothersole/GMC

Index